Bayesian Analysis with Excel and R

Conrad G. Carlberg

Contents at a Glance

Downloadable Bonus Content

Excel Worksheets

Book: *Statistical Analysis: Microsoft Excel 2016* (PDF)

To access bonus materials, please register your book at informit.com/register and enter ISBN 9780137580989.

T0292981

Bayesian Analysis with Excel and R

Editor-in-Chief
Mark Taub

Acquisitions Editor
Debra Williams Cauley

Development Editor
Chris Zahn

Managing Editor
Sandra Schroeder

Senior Project Editor
Tonya Simpson

Indexer
Timothy Wright

Proofreader
Donna E. Mulder

Technical Editors
Nick Cohron
Regina R. Monaco

Publishing Coordinator
Cindy Teeters

Cover Designer
Chuti Prasertsith

Compositor
CodeMantra

Warning and Disclaimer

Every effort has been made to make this book as complete and as accurate as possible, but no warranty or fitness is implied. The information provided is on an "as is" basis. The author and the publisher shall have neither liability nor responsibility to any person or entity with respect to any loss or damages arising from the information contained in this book.

Special Sales

For information about buying this title in bulk quantities, or for special sales opportunities (which may include electronic versions; custom cover designs; and content particular to your business, training goals, marketing focus, or branding interests), please contact our corporate sales department at corpsales@pearsoned.com or (800) 382-3419.

For government sales inquiries, please contact governmentsales@pearsoned.com.

For questions about sales outside the U.S., please contact intlcs@pearson.com.

Credits

Pearson's Commitment to Diversity, Equity, and Inclusion

Pearson is dedicated to creating bias-free content that reflects the diversity of all learners. We embrace the many dimensions of diversity, including but not limited to race, ethnicity, gender, socioeconomic status, ability, age, sexual orientation, and religious or political beliefs.

Education is a powerful force for equity and change in our world. It has the potential to deliver opportunities that improve lives and enable economic mobility. As we work with authors to create content for every product and service, we acknowledge our responsibility to demonstrate inclusivity and incorporate diverse scholarship so that everyone can achieve their potential through learning. As the world's leading learning company, we have a duty to help drive change and live up to our purpose to help more people create a better life for themselves and to create a better world.

Our ambition is to purposefully contribute to a world where:

- Everyone has an equitable and lifelong opportunity to succeed through learning.
- Our educational products and services are inclusive and represent the rich diversity of learners.
- Our educational content accurately reflects the histories and experiences of the learners we serve.
- Our educational content prompts deeper discussions with learners and motivates them to expand their own learning (and worldview).

While we work hard to present unbiased content, we want to hear from you about any concerns or needs with this Pearson product so that we can investigate and address them.

Please contact us with concerns about any potential bias at
https://www.pearson.com/report-bias.html.

Contents

Downloadable Bonus Content

Excel Worksheets

Book: *Statistical Analysis: Microsoft Excel 2016* (PDF)

To access bonus materials, please register your book at informit.com/register and enter ISBN 9780137580989.

About the Author

Conrad Carlberg is a nationally recognized expert on quantitative analysis, data analysis, and management applications such as Microsoft Excel, SAS, and Oracle. He holds a Ph.D. in statistics from the University of Colorado and is a many-time recipient of Microsoft's Excel MVP designation. He is the author of many books, including *Business Analysis with Microsoft Excel*, Fifth Edition, *Statistical Analysis: Microsoft Excel 2016*, *Regression Analysis Microsoft Excel*, and *R for Microsoft Excel Users*.

Carlberg is a Southern California native. After college he moved to Colorado, where he worked for a succession of startups and attended graduate school. He spent two years in the Middle East, teaching computer science and dodging surly camels. After finishing graduate school, Carlberg worked at US West (a Baby Bell) in product management and at Motorola.

In 1995 he started a small consulting business (www.conradcarlberg.com), which provides design and analysis services to companies that want to guide their business decisions by means of quantitative analysis—approaches that today we group under the term "analytics." He enjoys writing about those techniques and, in particular, how to carry them out using the world's most popular numeric analysis application, Microsoft Excel.

Preface

This book has several aspects that I want to let you know about up front. If you're already comfortable with terminology and concepts such as Hamiltonian Monte Carlo sampling, conjugate pairs, and posterior distributions, then this book is probably not for you. You already know a lot about those topics, and if you need more you know where to find it.

On the other hand, if you don't feel quite at home with the purpose of random samples, R's user interface, and why you might want to work with mean-corrected instead of with raw values, then it's just possible that this book offers something that you might want to know about. Both this book and I assume that you have some background in statistical analysis—say, at the introductory college level, where you can expect to study some probability theory and how it applies to the assessment of sample means, variances, and correlations. Particularly if you have studied these problems in the past, you will be better placed to understand how Bayesian analysis differs from traditional approaches, and how it works out in the context of the functions and packages found in R. And if you feel as though you could use some refresher work in traditional statistical analysis, Pearson is making available to you for download an e-book titled *Statistical Analysis: Microsoft Excel 2016*. You'll find details on obtaining that book at the end of this Preface.

You're experienced. You probably have something close to the background in Bayesian analysis that I had in mind when I laid out the topics that I wanted this book to cover. It seemed to me that the world already has plenty of books about statistics and experimental methodology: one more isn't going to help much. Something similar can be said about using syntax and diction that R recognizes: we already have as many elementary to intermediate texts on R as we need.

What we did need, I thought, was a source of information that connected the simplistic capabilities of VBA (the programming language historically offered by Microsoft Excel to give the user more control over the application) with the more sophisticated capabilities of programming languages such as R and C.

Similarly, we were missing information about three basic types of sampling that range from the simplistic, univariate sort of categorical analysis that you find in undergraduate texts to the complex sampling methods used by techniques such as quadratic approximation and Markov Chain Monte Carlo (MCMC). Richard McElreath has written, and has supplied to R, helper functions that ease the task of designing, writing, and installing the code that does the heavy lifting for you.

I have done what I can in this book to leverage the Excel skills that you have already developed in the areas of managing functions, handling data, and designing graphs and plots. The point will come that you see that Excel too handles the necessary tools of calculus in the form of function arguments—albeit more slowly and awkwardly. Shortly thereafter you'll see how the three fundamental approaches to building posterior distributions by sampling are in fact wonderfully creative solutions to the same problem.

Now let's see how I propose to get us there.

Chapter 1: Bayesian Analysis and R: An Overview

When I first approached Pearson about writing this book, I came away from the discussions just a little discouraged. The editors and their advisors were polite and really good at listening, but I didn't think that I heard much in the way of encouragement. In particular, they wanted to know why I would want to write this book.

Good question. I had several reasons in mind, but it wasn't easy to articulate them. Still, I did so, and apparently I did so successfully because, well, look at what you're holding. And those reasons made sense as a place to start out, but I'll keep it to the first two that occurred to me:

- Why would you want to read it? There are several reasons, but if you are like most of us you use Microsoft Excel for most numeric purposes, even though Excel was designed as a general-purpose calculation engine. You might have stayed away from Bayesian analysis because you heard that Excel is comparatively slow. And you're right: because of both software problems and hardware issues, there was a time when you had to wait and wait for a solution to the problem that you posed to Bayesian software. No longer. Now you can get an answer in a reasonable length of time, and without making assumptions that you don't feel quite comfortable with.

- People I work with were using familiar words in unfamiliar ways. They were using terms like *prior*, *likelihood*, and *parameter* in contexts that they did not seem to fit. I wanted to find out more about what they were saying. But I needed a starting point, and because I was quite familiar with Excel's numeric capabilities, I decided to work from the platform of Excel and toward a platform based on R. It's true that Excel is comparatively slow and doesn't have many functions that you would like to have in a Bayesian-oriented platform. But for certain problems, Excel works great and returns accurate results in a short timeframe. Fine; I can work from there.

That's what's going on in Chapter 1. Let's move ahead.

Chapter 2: Generating Posterior Distributions with the Binomial Distribution

The basic idea behind a Bayesian analysis is to create a posterior distribution that informs you about the parameters that bring about the results of the simulation. You do not want to start a sequence with one family of distributions and then try to finish the sequence in another family, so you should aim for a situation in which the prior and the likelihood are from the same family.

That, of course, implies that you select the distributional family from which the product will stem. You have several families from which to choose, but your choice will almost inevitably depend on the specific questions that you want to answer, which in turn depend on the nature of the data that you want to analyze.

One basic family of distributions is the binomial distribution. The term *binomial* itself implies the nature of a binomial distribution: two names, such as win and loss, buys and doesn't buy, survives and fails to survive, and so on. Consider your lifetime experience with coins. You have almost surely come to expect that when you pull a coin at random from your pocket and flip it, the probability is 50% that it will come up heads and 50% that it will come up tails. That's a binomial distribution: two names, two outcomes, two results.

The distinctive feature of a binomial distribution is that its values are discrete rather than continuous. When you flip the coin, you do not anticipate that the flip could come up with any of an infinite number of results. You anticipate two and only two outcomes, heads and tails.

This can be a very different situation from that of a person's height or weight. Then, each measurement is just one of an *infinite* number of possible heights or weights. The beta distribution, discussed in Chapter 3, is an example of a continuous distribution as distinct from a discrete one, such as the binomial. When you set up your analysis using R, for example, you can specify that a given parameter should be distributed as binomial, or any of R's distributional families. This flexibility is one characteristic that makes R's structure, and its design, so useful in Bayesian analysis.

Right here's a good spot to stress that it's important to specify the distributional characteristics of the parameters you use in an analysis, but don't let them blind you to other aspects—aspects that you might well ignore if you were to ignore all the good reasons for adding Bayes to your toolkit.

It's all too easy to forget that one of the key assumptions underlying a binomial test is that any two tests in your experiment are independent of one another. Suppose that you are studying the distribution of political party membership; one of the questions you ask is therefore which party, if any, a respondent belongs to.

To make a valid inference regarding the probability of a participant's response, you must be sure that the response is independent of any other response in your survey. So, the value of George's response must be unaffected by the value of Ellen's response. If that is the case, you're able to add and subtract subtotals directly (for example, to derive cumulative totals) without having to adjust for some probably unknowable dependency in the data.

Chapter 2 discusses this sort of concern in greater detail.

Chapter 3: Understanding the Beta Distribution

The principal difference between the binomial and the beta distribution is the degree of granularity with which variables are measured. Both distributions show how numeric variables are distributed across a span of values, much like the normal curve shows how a y-variable is distributed across a range of x-values.

But a variable that follows a beta distribution does so in a continuous rather than an interrupted fashion. The heads and tails left by coin flips follow a binomial pattern. Sorted by their actual values (heads, tails on a coin; 1, 2, 3,..., 6 on a die), the values that you see are not distributed continuously but discretely. We do not act as though a third of a head is a legitimate coin flip value, any more than we do that 2 1/2 is a legitimate value for the roll of a die.

But both those values would be legitimate if the variable, instead of being a coin flip or the roll of dice, were a plant's weight or height. Weight and height are both legitimately continuous variables, and each can take on an infinite number of values. That's the distinction between the distributions: if a distribution can take on any number of numeric values it's a beta, whereas a binomial distribution is limited typically to a much smaller number of values, such as 2 for a coin flip, 11 for a dice roll, and 2 if an item is judged defective or acceptable in a quality control context.

Both R and Excel have functions used to explore and manipulate the binomial *and* the beta distributions. It's useful to keep in mind that there are times when it's more convenient and just as quick to use Excel and VBA for generating frequency distributions as it is to use R. Chapter 4 has more to say about this matter.

Keep in mind that both Bayesian and frequentist approaches often return results that are either very close to one another (due to rounding errors induced by nearly all applications of calculus) or identical.

Chapter 4: Grid Approximation and the Beta Distribution

At this point, the discussion has centered on frequency distributions, both discrete (binomial) and continuous (beta). It moves now to the use of approximation techniques with frequency distributions.

Bayesian methods depend on approximations of distributions. We can, literally by fiat, declare that there exists a frequency distribution that is defined by its location (its mean) and its spread (variance or standard deviation). We can pass those attributes—the mean and the variance—to software that with adequate speed and efficiency builds the distribution we're after, with the required location and spread.

VBA can do that. We can use VBA to structure an array of values that, when populated with enough values, looks and behaves like a beta distribution or a binomial distribution or a normal distribution, or any other recognizable distribution of data. So how is it that VBA has acquired a reputation for slow and clumsy code?

An important part of the answer is that VBA is only partly compiled at runtime. It's an interpreted language, which means the same code must be compiled repeatedly, again slowing matters down. Furthermore, VBA is not optimized for array management; newer languages such as Python manage arrays much more effectively by converting multi-row, multi-column arrays to single-row vectors, which some insist speeds up processing dramatically.

This chapter demonstrates how a posterior distribution changes in response to the act of modifying the likelihood. It's a useful place to provide that demonstration because it shows how the grid approximation technique results in simple modifications to the frequency distribution's structure—and the rationale for terming it a grid approximation.

Chapter 5: Grid Approximation with Multiple Parameters

Issues such as the speed with which hardware executes instructions, the efficiency with which code fills a distribution with simulated data, whether the computer in use is a vector machine, and other considerations are unquestionably important to the speed with which an analysis runs. But generally, a more important issue is the number of parameters and quantiles you ask the analysis to deal with.

When you expect to analyze only one parameter, even if it has as many as seven or eight meaningful levels, you could push likelihoods through a Bayesian analysis and have plenty of time left over. It might seem obvious, but as soon as you add a parameter to the design, you aren't just adding but multiplying design cells.

Start with six levels of a parameter, which even BASIC code could analyze before you finish your coffee. Now add another parameter that has five levels, and you're not simulating record counts for just 6 + 5 = 11, but 6 * 5 = 30 design cells. You might never have to put a simulated record in one of those multiple parameter cells, depending on matters such as size of the standard deviation, but your grid approximation code will need to attend to every one of them, when a quadratic approximation or a Markov Chain Monte Carlo instead could go flying past them.

Chapter 5 will give you a sense of how much time is spent needlessly dealing with design cells just because grid approximation requires that they be there.

Chapter 6: Regression Using Bayesian Methods

Most of us are familiar with the regression approach to solving problems that are presented in the context of the general linear model. We're familiar, even comfortable, with a page or two of printed output that includes figures such as

- Traditional correlation coefficients and regression constants
- Regression summaries such as R^2
- Inferential statistics such as F ratios and standard errors of estimate

This chapter begins to tie together concepts and techniques that in previous chapters have remained largely isolated from one another. In particular, difficulties imposed by the grid approximation method can be painful, especially when multiple predictor variables are involved. There are various reasons for this, particularly when the experimenter wants to assess the simultaneous effect of multiple variables. If one can't evaluate the combined effects of water and fertilization on a crop, it's at least that difficult to evaluate their separate effects. But just when the experiment becomes really interesting due to the addition of variables, the analysis starts to groan under the weight of that addition.

Chapter 6 starts to replace the use of grid approximation with that of an R function named quap, or *quadratic approximation*. The reason that so much ink is spent on discussing grid approximation is that it forms the basis for more sophisticated techniques such as speeding up the structuring and populating of posterior distributions, faster methods of approximating posterior distributions than grid approximation. Furthermore, the extra speed of quadratic approximation enables us to use multiple predictor variables simultaneously—and without that capability, grid approximation falls short.

Like grid approximation, quap approximates the posterior distribution density of the parameters we want to know about. To do so, the software uses a quadratic function, so we term it a *quadratic approximation*.

Chapter 7: Handling Nominal Variables

Often you'll have a variable whose values have been saved as numeric values but that should be analyzed as though the numeric values were in fact text values. This chapter discusses ways to handle them so that text values are managed as though they were in fact numeric. The opposite approach, in which numeric values are handled as though they were text, also exists. Dummy coding and index variables are discussed here, as is the use of the quap function to make conversion more straightforward.

Chapter 8: MCMC Sampling Methods

The final chapter in this book moves to a technique that for several years has been the gold standard for Bayesian sampling: Markov Chain Monte Carlo, or MCMC. Other and older approaches tend to get stuck in particular thickets of the posterior distribution, often because of autocorrelation built into the sampling logic. But MCMC manages to avoid that trap, and to simultaneously maintain its execution speed.

That characteristic—maintaining speed while increasing design complexity—is what allows MCMC to simulate large posterior distributions without slowing down unduly. In turn, that positions you to code predictor variables so that they behave in the best ways of both continuous and discrete variables, and in ways that ease their interpretation when it comes time to evaluate the results.

Who Are Those Guys?

Right about now you might well be asking yourself, "Why should I read this? What kind of statistical analysis is the author pushing, Bayesian or frequentist?" The best I can do by way of an answer to those questions is to tell you a little bit about my education and experience.

I took my first course in statistical analysis at a small, well-regarded liberal arts college in the Midwest. It was a miserable experience, and that might well have been due to the fact that it was taught out of the psychology department. I still have the textbook that was used in that course, and in the fashion of the day (this was in the 1970s) it told its readers what to do with a bunch of numbers and almost nothing about why it made sense to do that.

Nevertheless, I finished that course in statistics and took a couple more just for good measure. They were a bit better than the one I took from the psych department. After my undergrad degree I enrolled in grad school and started out under a professor who I knew I wanted to study with. He was a frequentist and was first author on a basic statistics text that broke new ground: It explained to the reader *why* it was desirable to include certain calculations in a given statistical analysis.

His book, as well as his classes, stressed the rationale for the kinds of analysis that were *de rigueur* during the late 1970s. You followed up carefully designed experiments with tests of statistical significance. You used t-tests (Gossett) to calculate that statistical significance with two groups. You used the analysis of variance (Fisher) to calculate that statistical significance with more than two groups. You used the product-moment correlation coefficient (Pearson) to measure the strength of the relationship between two ratio variables. You used factor analysis and multivariate analysis of variance (Green; Wilks) to reduce a data overload down to a few manageable factors and to test differences between groups measured on more than one outcome variable. You used multiple comparisons (Tukey) to pinpoint the location of statistically significant differences between group means.

Every one of these techniques belongs in the frequentist toolkit. I used each of them, in combination with an ad hoc technique called exponential smoothing, at a large telecommunications firm during the 1980s. We were able to reduce a bloated resale inventory from more than $14 million to less than $7 million in under a year, without write downs. (This was back when $14 million was a lot of money.)

So I have every possible reason in my educational and professional background to be grateful for the tools that frequentist statistics has offered me. And I am grateful. But...

I start to feel uneasy every time I read about a finding by the Reproducibility Project that contradicts the finding of another published study. That can happen, and does, for reasons that range from mis-specifying a design so that it treats a random factor as fixed, to something as commonplace as p-hacking.

I worry when I find that someone has applied Welch's correction or something similar in a situation where sample sizes are unequal and so are population variances: the Behrens-Fisher problem. There's something wrong with a scientific approach that allows such a problem to exist so long without a satisfactory solution.

The analysis of variance (ANOVA) has the principal purpose of determining whether any two population means are equal in an experiment consisting of at least three groups. There are at least six distinct procedures, collectively called *multiple comparisons*, intended to pinpoint which groups are responsible for a significant ANOVA outcome. One of them requires a standardized score difference of 7.5 for two means to be considered significantly different at the .05 level, and another requires a difference of 15. It is true that our choice of multiple comparison procedure differs according to the situation under which the data were collected and given the inferences we want to make. Still, we should be able to come up with methods that agree more closely than do the Scheffé and planned orthogonal contrasts.

Then there's multicollinearity, an issue that crops up in regression analysis. It can pose other problems for statistical analysis, and I touch on them briefly in Chapter 6. There are plenty of other similar issues, I promise you that. Some are solved by recourse to Bayesian methods, and some just aren't. My point is that I have no special reason to prefer frequentist methods to Bayesian or vice versa. I have tried in this book to avoid any bias toward frequentist methods, and I hope and think that I have succeeded.

Where to Find It

I suspect that you are someone who uses the R application with some level of experience. As such, I assume that you have probably installed R software on your computer, following the instructions provided by the CRAN website (cran.r-project.org). When you do so, quite a bit of default code and simple straightforward functions such as max and read.csv are automatically installed on your computer.

Other code takes the form of *packages*, and here there's nothing automatic about the installation. If you want to install a package, and you almost certainly will, the standard procedure is to identify a mirror site from the drop-down list that appears when you select the *Set CRAN mirror* item in R's *Packages* menu. After you have identified a mirror site, you can select one of the roughly 15,000 packages that CRAN offers in a drop-down.

Even though the packages are presented in alphabetical order, selecting one of 15,000 is more than most users look forward to doing. So you'll be glad to know that you do not need to go through that tedious process more than once in order to install the code discussed in this book.

> **NOTE** The R application, without any special assistance, recognizes most of the code discussed in this book. There are a few functions (notably, quap and ulam) that require you to install a package named *rethinking*. You do not use R's *Packages* menu to install *rethinking*. See Appendix A for detailed instructions on installing the *rethinking* package on a Windows machine.

And speaking of platforms, at the time that I'm writing this book, no provision is made to install *rethinking* on a Mac. For the time being, as far as we know, there is no version of *rethinking* that is compatible with the Mac.

At this point you should be good to go. Chapter 1, "Bayesian Analysis and R: An Overview," is coming right up.

Bonus Material

To access the downloadable worksheets and PDF of the book *Statistical Analysis: Microsoft Excel 2016* please

1. Got to informit.com/register.
2. Enter the ISBN 9780137580989.
3. Answer the proof of purchase challenge questions.
4. Click on the "Access Bonus Content" link in the Registered Products section of your account page, to be taken to the page where your downloadable content is available.

Bayesian Analysis and R: An Overview

1

When I first started reading what some people have to say about Bayesian analysis—and what others have to say about traditional statistical inference—I couldn't help recalling what Will Rogers had to say about partisan politics: "I'm not a member of any organized political party. I'm a Democrat."

Certainly, those who favor the Bayesian approach can marshal some strong arguments on their own behalf, as can their counterparts, the *frequentists*. And yet the statistician Sir Ronald Fisher, who is thought of as the premier frequentist, intemperately wrote that Bayesian theory " ... is founded upon an error and must be wholly rejected."

> **NOTE**
>
> Writers often refer to those who use and applaud Bayesian techniques as *Bayesians*, and to those who have developed and supported techniques such as Fisher (ANOVA), Gossett (t-tests), and Pearson (the Pearson correlation coefficient) as *frequentists*. I'll follow that approach in this book.

The strange thing is that many of the thought patterns and the analysis techniques that we think of today as frequentist are rooted in Bayesian theory. Some 500 years ago, gamblers were seeking an edge in casinos by using methods that today we would tend to think of more as Bayesian than frequentist. Around the year 1900, techniques stressing the differences between means, the use of standard deviations, correlations, and z-scores were getting emphasis.

Bayes Comes Back

Then, toward the end of the twentieth century, Bayesian methods made a comeback. Improvements in Bayesian theory helped, but what really moved things along was the development of relatively cheap computing power on the desktop. Bayesian techniques that are required include the assembly of frequency distributions that show the number of people (or orioles, or catalytic converters) that have a given characteristic (such as particular cholesterol levels, or pink feathers, or costs of goods sold).

Designing and structuring those frequency distributions takes time—both elapsed and inside the computer—but you need them if you are to make comparisons between samples and theoretical populations. That's just one way that frequentist and Bayesian analysis share strategies. The frequentist analysis of variance, for example, asks you to imagine a population that is distributed according to the assumptions made by the null hypothesis—and imagining such distributions takes just a moment or two.

Bayesians share that strategy, but only to a degree. Bayesian analyses ask you not only to imagine distributions but also to actually *build* them, so that you can count the number of cases who are male, who have registered as Democrats, whose annual income is $70,000, who are married, who live in Oregon, who have never tested positive for COVID-19—you get the idea. By the time you have accounted for the percent of the population of interest that occupies all the intersections of interest (e.g., sex by political party by income by marital status by state of residence by pandemic status), you already have to budget for thousands of design cells in the joint probability distribution (one cell for male Democrats who are unmarried and make between $25,000 and $30,000 who live in Missouri and have never been exposed to COVID, another cell for female Democrats who ... again, you get the idea).

That's no big deal when you're interested in studying only a couple of variables—say, sex and political preference. Depending on how you define your variables, you might have just six cells in the joint distribution: two sexes across three political parties. But if you're going to build a full simulation, with all the variables that might rationally impact a political preference, you need to account for each intersection of each variable in the design. And to do so in a reasonable amount of time takes coding strategies and chip speeds that simply weren't available before, say, the 1990s.

Coding languages such as R help a lot, although you can give them an assist by putting faster chips to work on your desktop. And for some univariate problems, the simpler approaches work just fine: when there are only a few design cells to fill, you can complete the simulation in a flash. This book describes one of those simpler methods, *grid approximation*, in its earlier chapters, particularly Chapter 4, "Grid Approximation and the Beta Distribution." The idea is not to sell you on grid approximation as a means of generating a frequency distribution but rather to introduce you to some of the ideas and strategies that underlie Bayesian analysis.

Another, somewhat more sophisticated, approach called *quadratic approximation* is designed to cope with more complex simulations. You'll find a more detailed discussion of the

Bayesian approach to regression analysis in Chapter 6, "Regression Using Bayesian Methods," which relies heavily on simulation via quadratic approximation in preference to grid approximation. When the design of the analysis is at all complicated, you'll find that approximating a posterior distribution via quadratic approximation is meaningfully faster than grid approximation. (The reason for the term *quadratic* is also in Chapter 6.) Quadratic approximation tends to result in posterior distributions that are very nearly Gaussian in shape. That's great if you're studying variables that tend to shape into normal curves when plotted. It turns out that most things that we care about, that we measure and count, are distributed in just that way.

> **NOTE** A posterior distribution occurs when you combine a prior distribution with a "likelihood" or "the data."

Yet a third method of deriving a posterior distribution is Markov Chain Monte Carlo (MCMC), which is not limited to small designs, as is grid approximation, nor is MCMC as insistently normal in its posteriors as are quadratic distributions. This book's final chapter takes a look at R's ulam function, which, with a little preparation on your behalf, creates code in R's language that enables R's *RStan* code to carry out the sampling and returns to you the posterior findings that you're after.

The question remains: "Why bother?" If we're still in the third decade of the 21st century, then you presumably have already studied how to tell whether the difference between two or more sample averages is a reliable one. You know what multiple regression is about, why standard deviations and variances matter, and how to manage regression when the dependent variable counts occurrences rather than comparing averages. Both Bayesian and frequentist approaches often return the same results. Why should you bother with approximations and Monte Carlo simulations when you already have the tools you need close at hand? Just click the Data Analysis button on Excel's Data tab.

Well, part of the reason is that some datasets just don't comply with some analysis techniques. A good example is the problem of multicollinearity. That comes about in, for example, multiple regression analysis, when two or more predictor variables are perfectly correlated with one another, or very nearly so. Then the techniques of matrix algebra, which was in extensive use for years, failed because certain matrices could not be inverted. The result was that you would get nonsense such as negative R^2 values.

So software developers virtually abandoned this approach to multiple regression in favor of a technique termed *QR decomposition*. This helped a little, but not enough, because the resolution of the problem relied on artificially setting the coefficient for one or more predictor variables to the constant value of zero. Or you could just throw your hands in the air and give up.

The Bayesian approach gets you past this obstacle because it does not rely on matrix algebra to compute its solution. But that obstacle doesn't come about all that often, so by itself it's a poor reason to discard least squares regression. A much sounder rationale is that frequentist approaches ask you to *imagine* the appearance of the population distributions from which the samples are taken. It's conceivable that you could wind up with samples that are normally distributed but taken from populations that are highly skewed.

In contrast, Bayesian approaches do not ask you to imagine the shape of population distributions, but rather ask you to build those distributions by means of sophisticated sampling methods.

Now that we have tools such as MCMC on the desktop, there is little reason *not* to run both a frequentist and a Bayesian analysis on the same datasets. If you do so, you get the benefits of radically different approaches to solving the problems of comparing means, evaluating variances, and assessing correlations. You get the benefits of confirmation without having to wait forever for the software to draw sensible samples.

But I admit that the most compelling personal reason I've come across to adopt Bayesian techniques results from a phone conversation I once had with a consultant. The topic of the Analysis of Covariance came up and he pointed out that grad schools weren't teaching ANCOVA any longer—everyone was teaching multi-level modeling instead. You don't have to hit me over the head with a sledgehammer.

About Structuring Priors

One of the difficulties involved with Bayesian analysis, whether in R or elsewhere, is sampling from the posterior—after you've designed and populated it—but also from large, strong, complex priors. (I'll get further into the distinctions between prior, likelihood, and posterior distributions in Chapters 2 and 3.) Several algorithms to drive the sampling inputs have been developed, all with particular strengths and defects. Their strengths are generally clear, but their defects can be fairly subtle. One such is autocorrelation, which tends to get the sampling algorithm stuck in a particular corner of the sampling space—a drawback of quadratic approximation. Most are derivations of older (but far from inferior) methods such as Metropolis sampling, and their abbreviated names suggest it; for example, the Gibbs sampler gave rise to BUGS (Bayes Using Gibbs Sampling) and JAGS (Just Another Gibbs Sampler).

The field is changing so rapidly that I don't propose to go into all the details and differences among the samplers. At present, the most generally sound and speediest method is Hamiltonian Monte Carlo (HMC), and we'll let ulam (an R function that helps structure HMC samples) do its work in optimizing the inputs so that the best sampling method available is chosen.

Watching the Jargon

When I first started reading about Bayesian analysis I was disconcerted to find that the written sources used some terms as though everyone would know what they meant. But I *didn't* know. Perhaps it was just my relentlessly frequentist upbringing. (More likely, I didn't bring the degree of discipline to my learning that I should have.) But whatever the reason, I got myself tied up in knots until I found a text that, in straightforward terms, explained the distinction between *probability density* and *probability mass* (or just *density* and *mass*). The authors of all the other texts apparently assumed that their readers already understood the distinction, or that its meaning was perfectly obvious.

At any rate, I promised myself that if I ever got a chance to explain those terms up front I'd do so. And it turns out that they're not as arcane as they might be. Figure 1.1 shows an example, one that will be familiar to anyone with more than a smattering of the basics of traditional statistics.

Figure 1.1
Mass represents an area. Density represents a distance.

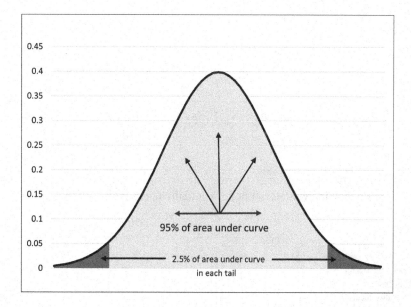

Figure 1.1 illustrates two different ways to conceptualize the amount of area under the curve. The horizontal arrows each point at a wedge that's at one tail of the curve. Together, the wedges account for 5% of the curve's area. Between the two wedges, and extending up from the curve's baseline, falls the remaining 95% of the curve's area. The probability is 95% that a randomly selected item will occupy a portion of the area between the two wedges. That area is termed the *mass*. R has functions such as `dbeta` and `dbinom` that make it quick and reasonably easy to assemble and analyze distributions based on both continuous (e.g., height) and discrete (e.g., dice) data.

Now have a look at Figure 1.2.

The underlying data is different from Figure 1.1, but the important point is that both figures illustrate mass measurements. Figure 1.1 has three areas with mass: 2.5%, 95%, and 2.5%; Figure 1.2 displays one mass, accounting for 100% of the distribution. A plot with different underlying data, such as a histogram with several columns of different sizes, could have several mass measurements, one for each column.

Figure 1.2
This curve has one mass: the entire region below the curve.

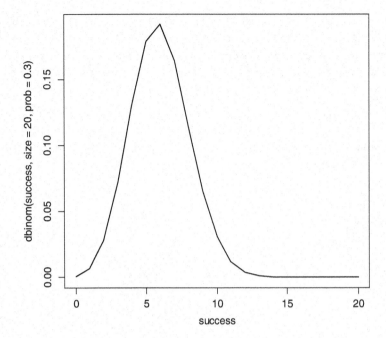

But in Figure 1.3, although there are 26 individual data points, the probability of the occurrence of any individual data point is initially unclear.

Figure 1.3
The densities represent the relative probabilities well, but they are uninformative about any probability masses that might be of interest.

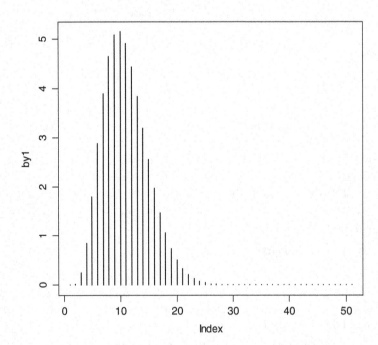

We do not have a value that tells us the width of each column, and consequently we can't determine the area covered by each column. Bayesian analysis often refers to Figure 1.3 as a *density distribution*. The density will usually tell you the height of each column *relative to the heights of the other columns* and, in turn, that can help you explore the full distribution's mode. (The mode rather than the median or mean, because the mode will often—not always, but often, as you'll see—represent the maximum a priori estimate in the distribution.) Figures 1.4 and 1.5 illustrate that you get the same results from dbeta and dbinom when probabilities are the same, in which the second and third arguments set the function's alpha and beta. The more equally spaced x-values you have in a binomial distribution, the more closely its shape conforms to a beta distribution that has the same probabilities. There are 501 values in both Figure 1.4 and Figure 1.5, and it's nearly impossible to distinguish them visually.

Figure 1.4
This distribution is drawn using the beta function.

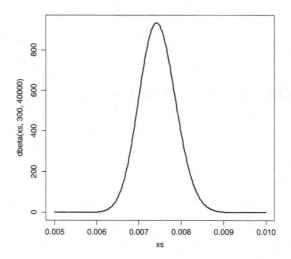

Figure 1.5
This distribution is drawn using the binom function.

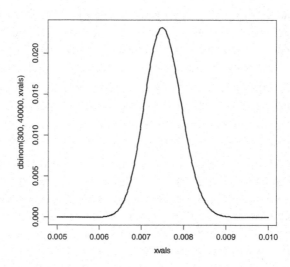

The analogous worksheet functions in Excel are `BINOM.DIST`, `BINOM.INV`, `BETA.DIST`, and `BETA.INV`. I suggest that you experiment with both the R versions and the Excel versions to see the effect of the probabilities and shapes on the distributions. Sample R code for the binomial chart is as follows:

```
xvals <- seq (0.005,0.01,by=0.00001)
plot(xvals,dbinom(300,40000,xvals),type='l',lwd=3)
```

and for the beta chart the sample code is

```
xvals <- seq (0.005,0.01,by=0.00001)
plot(xvals,dbeta(xvals,300,40000),type='l',lwd=3)
```

You'll learn more about this in subsequent chapters, but for now keep in mind that you can derive the relative density of each x value shown in a density distribution by totaling the x values and then dividing each by their total. This process is termed *standardizing* (occasionally, *normalizing*), and it's really no more than determining the percentage of total density that's accounted for by each x value.

Priors, Likelihoods, and Posteriors

Most basic Bayesian analyses, such as those discussed in this book, manipulate data that is found in three distributions:

- The prior distribution
- The likelihood
- The posterior distribution

As you'll see, these three distributions follow one another, both logically and on the clock.

The Prior

Typically, you specify the prior distribution's number of observations, their mean, and their variance. You combine the prior's data with the data that you collect from the likelihood, and that combination determines the posterior distribution. The posterior distribution can become, then, the prior distribution for the next cycle.

You might run through that cycle several times. It's helpful to remember that you do not need to supply raw data, case by case, to the software that carries out the analysis. R provides functions that enable you to specify the summary statistics such as count, mean, and variance as of any iteration in the process.

A prior distribution (or more usually just a *prior*) is a data set that has come about through standard operating procedures that might, or might not, be generally known. For example, a company might decide to determine the type of operating system in use when a potential customer logs onto its site. If there are three popular operating systems, the company's website might decide to mark up a particular product by 5%, another part by 10%, and one by 15%, depending on the user's operating system. It would not necessarily be clear to you, or to anyone for that matter, that the company's retail prices were being set in that fashion.

In that case, you or anyone might be entirely justified in assuming that differences in product performance had everything to do with market forces, and little or nothing to do with market or sales management. But if you can get your hands on generally accepted information regarding the products' performance in light of their revenues, that might be a good place to start with your prior.

Priors come in different forms. The acquisition of the data in a prior is normally followed by another acquisition of data, usually termed *likelihood*. If a prior has so much information in it that the addition of more data, in the form of a likelihood, will make little difference to the way the data is distributed, that's a strong prior.

If a prior has relatively little data in it—relative, that is, to the amount of data in the likelihood—that's a weak prior. For example, the strong prior usually has so much raw data in it that subsequent data in the form of the likelihood is swallowed up. The reverse can of course occur.

Both frequentists and many Bayesians have long and fiercely objected to the apparent subjectivity involved in specifying priors. Mathematicians and scientists have disagreed, often contentiously, about whether it is appropriate for an analyst to get directly involved in their specification. This book will not settle arguments between, for example, Laplace and Keynes. But you should be aware that theorists have found plenty here to disagree on.

Another aspect of priors to bear in mind is whether a prior is in the same distribution family as the posterior distribution. If so, the prior is called the *conjugate prior to the likelihood*. It's difficult to complete the Bayesian cycle of events when the prior and the likelihood belong to different distributional families and the prior and the posterior are therefore not conjugates.

The noninformative prior also has a place in this structure. Suppose that you were confronted by a problem that has no generally accepted solution. You would like to establish a prior before collecting data concerning the problem, but because there is no generally accepted solution, you want to avoid a solution based on one. The usual way to do so is to place a constant 1 in the prior across its range, and that results in a density chart of the prior that consists only of a straight line. You cannot design a weaker prior than that. It may well be that the prior doesn't conform to the way that the world works, and in fact you wind up choosing an outcome willy-nilly when that's exactly what you want to avoid doing.

Some problems are best left alone.

The Likelihood

The second of the three standard, conceptual steps that you take in carrying out a Bayesian analysis is most frequently termed the *likelihood* or the *data* (although neither term is well-suited to the term *step*). The data step is taken after the prior has been defined and structured, and, quite likely, populated.

1

The rationale for using the term *likelihood* in this context is a little weak, but here it is. After outset of the analysis, when the prior has been specified, you have at least two possibilities: that the prior is true and that the prior is false. The likelihood gets into matters when you take the prior into account.

Suppose that the prior is true. Then there is a probability of observing an outcome when the prior is true as well as a probability that applies when the prior is false. This is where the notion of *likelihood* comes in. Suppose the prior has it that a condition is true 90% of the time. Then the probability that the second step is true is termed the *likelihood*.

Furthermore, the prior might also have it that the condition is true 80% of the time. You can calculate the probability that the second step is true, and what's more, you can compare those two probabilities to determine which probability is greater—that is, the *maximum likelihood*. Hence the term "likelihood" to specify the likelihood of that second step.

That chain of etymological logic is a little trappy, and plenty of Bayesians prefer to use the term *data* rather than *likelihood*. The *posterior* distribution is the result of combining the prior with the likelihood. It's possible—even typical—to simply add the prior distribution to the likelihood. The posterior distribution is often the end point of the three-step process, but not necessarily.

For example, you might have arrived at a posterior distribution but you haven't yet finished the process of data acquisition and compilation. It's easy enough to treat the existing posterior distribution as a new prior, and then to compile that new prior with a new likelihood to generate a new posterior. In Chapter 4, Figures 4.1 through 4.7 provide an example of that process.

This is an example of the desirability of conjugate pairs, which I discuss in no great detail in Chapter 4 as part of the beta distribution. Suppose that you started out with a prior from a normal distribution. If you subsequently found yourself trying to combine that prior with a likelihood from the uniform distribution, you might find yourself in trouble. A uniform distribution cannot successfully be combined as discussed earlier in this chapter with a normal distribution: they are not from the same family of distributions.

Contrasting a Frequentist Analysis with a Bayesian

Let's take a look at a fairly straightforward example of how a frequentist and a Bayesian might go about analyzing the prospects of an election to the U.S. Senate. The idea here is to give you a sense of the differences between how they think about the problem as well as differences in the tools that they bring to bear on it. It's surprising how complicated a frequentist analysis can be, even when the research question itself is simple.

This election is not fraught with problems such as tie breaks and hanging chads; there are only two candidates. The question boils down to which candidate attracted more votes than the other candidate. A poll of 100 eligible voters finds that 20% of respondents favor Candidate A—a clear minority. But is the sample of 100 voters large enough, and is Candidate A trailing by so much that they might just as well withdraw today?

The Frequentist Approach

This section is not intended to discuss all the procedural niceties associated with testing a sample mean against a hypothetical mean. That will come later. (In the meantime, you might want to check out what the e-book made available by the publisher has to say about t-tests and z-tests.) For now, I just want to make you aware of some of the differences between the frequentist and the Bayesian approaches.

Here is how a frequentist might think. The result of the poll, 20% in favor of Candidate A, represents a sample of the electorate, and as long as the approved voting procedures are followed, each vote is independent of every other vote in this sample. In that case, the central limit theorem applies, and we can regard the sample mean as an observation from an imaginary distribution: a normal curve.

With that set of data and some assumptions, we can construct a *confidence interval* around the 20% poll result. That confidence interval might extend from, say, a lower boundary of 5% and an upper boundary of 35%, with a midpoint of 20%. Because of the central limit theorem, we know that if we conducted the poll many times, Candidate A's support *could* range anywhere from 0% to 100% on all those imaginary polls. But our best estimate of Candidate A's support is 20%: the amount returned by the poll that was actually taken. So let's build a confidence interval around that 20% point.

The breadth of that confidence interval is a function of two other figures: the value of Candidate A's score, 20%, and how confident the analyst wants to be that the interval captures some criterion value, say, 95%. In other words, we want to know the frequency of the imaginary sample means that surround the 20% point and that fall between the lower and the upper limits of the confidence interval. To get the limits of the confidence interval, we first need the standard error of the candidate's poll score:

> Standard error = s / $\sqrt{n}$

where:

> *s* is the standard deviation of the 100 votes
>
> *n* is the number of votes

And in this case, the standard error equals 0.04.

Now multiply the standard error by the z-scores that represent the 2.5% and 97.5% percentile points in the normal curve. Note that this tells us the number of standard errors below and above 20% where the limits of the 95% confidence interval are located. In z-score units, the limits of the confidence interval are +/− 1.96. When you multiply the standard error by the z-score units, you get a confidence interval of 0.12 to 0.28. Specifically, 0.20 − 0.8 = 0.12 and 0.20 + 0.8 = 0.28.

So, if Candidate A is the choice of 20% of the voting population (and on the basis of a single poll that's our best estimate), he or she should probably pull out of the race immediately.

We are 95% confident that between 12% and 28% of the electorate will wind up voting for Candidate A. Somehow, he or she would have to boost that 28% up to 50%, and that's not an easy task.

You can test all this with Excel's Data Analysis add-in, using its Descriptive Statistics tool (even though confidence intervals are inferential, rather than descriptive, tools).

Bear in mind that a test such as the one described in this section is among the easiest in the frequentist's inferential toolkit to carry out. But I have not even mentioned issues such as whether you know the population variance or whether this sample is large enough to sensibly choose between a t-test and a z-test, choosing between a directional and a non-directional test, interpreting the probabilities associated with confidence intervals, and the joint effects of sample sizes and variances on the resulting probabilities.

And yet it's the easiest inferential statistical test around. Let's move on to the Bayesian version.

The Bayesian Approach

Now, what would a Bayesian analyst do when faced with the same problem that the frequentist faced at the start of this section? The Bayesian would call on the R application to run code like the following:

```
library(rethinking)
grid <- seq( from=0 , to=1 , length.out=1000 )
prior <- rep(1,1000)
likelihood <- dbinom( x = 20 , size = 100 , prob = grid )
posterior <- likelihood * prior
posterior <- posterior / sum(posterior)
poll_means <- sample( grid , size = 1000 , replace = TRUE , prob  =
 posterior )
PI( poll_means , prob=0.95 )
```

The code consists of six functions, as follows:

The `library` function draws R's attention to the `rethinking` package, which contains the code needed to run the `PI` (percentile intervals) function.

The `seq` function establishes a sequence of 1000 numbers ranging from zero to 1, with each number 1 one-thousandth greater than the preceding number. When populated, this grid will contain the number of sample means that equal a particular value in the grid.

The `rep` function establishes a vector of 1000 instances of the numeral 1.

The `dbinom` function returns to *likelihood* the probability of (in this example) observing a value of 1 in a vector of 100 votes that contains 20 ones, with an intrinsic probability defined by the sequence in *grid*.

The *posterior* is initiated by multiplying *likelihood* by *prior*.

The *posterior* is standardized by dividing each *likelihood* value by the sum of its values.

The `sample` function draws 1000 sample means from *grid*, replacing each value after it has been sampled, with a probability found in the *posterior*.

The `PI` function establishes a 95% confidence interval around the poll's mean of 0.2. (Notice that although Excel's Data Analysis add-in reports half the width of the confidence interval, the PI function reports the PI limits themselves.)

When you run the sequence of instructions just given, R responds with the limits of a 95% percentile interval around the value of x (here, 0.2). With these data, the percentile interval extends from 0.13 to 0.29, very close to those produced with the help of Excel, 0.12 and 0.28.

Although the results of the two analyses just given are very close to one another, they were obtained by two very different methods. Both approaches require us to deal with an imaginary distribution, but the frequentist's distribution is entirely imaginary, whereas the Bayesian distribution is not: it is a simulation.

The frequentist method relies on the central limit theorem to justify comparing a sample poll mean with a wholly made-up sampling distribution. It uses the standard error in that sampling distribution to calculate the size of the confidence interval. We don't measure the standard error directly. These statistics and concepts (the central limit theorem, the standard error of the mean, and so forth) are frequently shown to be valid, albeit usually by demonstration rather than by means of formal proof.

It is true that the results of a frequentist analysis are seldom precisely equal to those returned via a Bayesian analysis, although it is also true that the two forms of analysis generally return similar results. This outcome is often due to minor differences in the way that calculus is deployed. (But bear in mind that no part of this book requires the use of calculus: it's hidden inside the black box.) Those differences can also be due to the fact that the analysis requires sampling in order to create simulated distributions. Frequentist or Bayesian, much depends on how the sample is taken.

Summary

This chapter has several purposes. First and most important, I wanted to discuss some terminology that is probably unfamiliar, even in the familiar context of frequentist statistics. It's just not feasible to discuss these concepts without clarifying their meanings in a Bayesian context.

I also wanted to start applying those concepts around a rationale for using Bayesian statistics. It's not reasonable to ask you to use a largely new way of thinking without explaining its purpose. I'm by no means up to that. But now that we've cleared some terminological underbrush out of the way, we can move on to discussing how concepts such as priors and likelihoods interact with distributions to bring about useful results.

We'll take a look at how the prior, the likelihood, and the posterior distribution work in concert with the binomial distribution in Chapter 2.

Generating Posterior Distributions with the Binomial Distribution

2

Bayesian analysis makes use of a variety of tools that are needed for special situations; for example, the Metropolis algorithm and a type of Metropolis algorithm called Gibbs sampling. But you can count on most instances of Bayesian analysis to depend on three structures: the prior distribution, the data (also termed *likelihood*), and the posterior distribution. This chapter discusses how you can make use of the binomial distribution to generate these structures.

Unfortunately, more than one name is used for each of these structures. I call the situation "unfortunate" because it complicates already complicated concepts. For example, *data* is a term used in Bayesian analysis that is also often called the *likelihood*. The prior distribution is often known simply as *the prior*, and you'll also see terms such as *beliefs* and *conjectures* used as synonyms for the prior distribution. In this book I try to keep to the three terms used in the preceding paragraph: prior, likelihood, and posterior.

Bayesian analysis combines the prior with the likelihood so as to result in a posterior. It does so by applying Bayes' theorem:

$$P(A \mid B) = P(A) \, P(B \mid A) \; / \; P(B)$$

of which both this chapter and the entire book have more to say. For now though, it's enough to know this:

- P(A) is the probability that event A occurs
- P(B) is the probability that event B occurs
- P(A | B) is the probability that event A occurs, conditioned on event B
- P(B | A) is the probability that event B occurs, conditioned on event A

This symbol:

|

(often termed a "pipe symbol") is used in the context of probability analysis to mean "conditioned on" or "given that" or some similar phrase that alters the context of the event. For example, you could refer to the event that a particular person is a registered Democrat as *event A*, and the event that a particular person is male as *event B*. In that case, P(A) might be 40% and P(B) might be 45%. And P(A | B) would mean the probability that a person is a Democrat, given that the person is male.

Bayesian analysis usually involves the combination of probabilities in this fashion, and because probabilities are based on counts of event occurrences, the analysis is often concerned with the combinations of those counts. That's what it means to combine the prior with the data. The prior is a distribution of counts across different categories. That distribution is frequently a raw estimate of counts within categories, or the probabilities that arise from those counts, and is frequently no better than a guess. It's particularly likely to be a guess if you are just starting to investigate a particular phenomenon.

Suppose that the year is 2020, and you're starting to investigate the prevalence of the COVID-19 virus in the United States. With nothing to go on but some educated guesses, you might define a prior for the United States' daily cases as 30,000 existing cases.

When the next count becomes available, you could add to the existing prior the new cases (the likelihood) to arrive at a posterior. Or if you were working with percentages you could combine the prior with the data by multiplying them together—again, reaching a new posterior. When new data becomes available, that posterior might well become the new prior.

Either way, when you're basing your analysis on a simple grid approximation, you're likely to be working with the binomial distribution—gets sick versus stays well, wears a mask versus doesn't, is versus isn't hospitalized. (Chapter 4 discusses grid approximation in more detail.) So it helps to be comfortable with the binomial distribution and the analytic tools for dealing with it.

Understanding the Binomial Distribution

Several different kinds of distributions, such as the normal distribution—that's the familiar bell curve—show the proportion of a population that has an amount of some attribute, such as height, blood pressure, and miles traveled in a car for each gallon of gasoline used. For example, "34% of United States males are between 70 and 72 inches tall. Another 34% are between 72 and 74 inches." Both these statements make use of our knowledge of the normal distribution.

Both Excel and R, along with various other applications, support the use of several types of distribution, including the normal and the binomial distributions.

Excel offers support for the use of the binomial distribution mostly by means of two worksheet functions, BINOM.DIST and BINOM.INV. Their syntax is as follows:

```
BINOM.DIST(number_s,trials,probability_s,cumulative)
BINOM.INV(trials,probability_s,alpha)
```

The BINOM.DIST function returns what's usually called the distribution's *probability mass function*, or *PMF*. It's characterized by the use of a given number of trials and a given probability of an event, such as 50% for a fair coin flip. You'll meet the PMF's close cousin, the *probability density function*, in the next chapter.

> **NOTE** Several other distributions, such as the beta, the Poisson, and the uniform distribution, are important in both Bayesian analysis and in traditional frequentist methods. This chapter and the next discuss the binomial and beta distributions, and this book describes additional distributions as they come up in an analysis.

Figure 2.1
Ten flips of a fair coin don't necessarily result in five heads and five tails.

	E5		fx	=BINOM.DIST(B5,$B$1,$B$2,$B$3)	
	A	B	C	D	E
1	Number of flips	10			
2	Coin's probability of comng up Heads	50%			
3	Cumulative probability	TRUE			Probability of
4	Distribution of 10 flips	Heads	Tails		number of heads
5		10	0	Probability of 10 heads in 10 flips:	100.00%
6		9	1	Probability of 9 heads in 10 flips:	99.90%
7		8	2	Probability of 8 heads in 10 flips:	98.93%
8		7	3	Probability of 7 heads in 10 flips:	94.53%
9		6	4	Probability of 6 heads in 10 flips:	82.81%
10		5	5	Probability of 5 heads in 10 flips:	62.30%
11		4	6	Probability of 4 heads in 10 flips:	37.70%
12		3	7	Probability of 3 heads in 10 flips:	17.19%
13		2	8	Probability of 2 heads in 10 flips:	5.47%
14		1	9	Probability of 1 heads in 10 flips:	1.07%
15		0	10	Probability of 0 heads in 10 flips:	0.10%

Figure 2.1 shows the binomial distribution in practice. You have a fair coin, which means that it is as likely to come up heads as tails on a given flip. The probability of heads (and tails, for that matter) is therefore a constant, shown in cell B2 of Figure 2.1. (That's the reason for the use of the term *binomial*, by the way. The *bi* prefix means "two" and the suffix *nomial* refers to "names," and here we have two names: heads and tails.)

And although you're using a fair coin, that doesn't necessarily mean that every set of ten flips results in five heads and five tails. Just sheer luck, or differences in how you strike the coin with your thumbnail, or how long you let the coin hang in the air before you catch it, or any of many other unmeasured variables, can result in a set of ten flips with more or fewer than five heads.

So there are 11 possible outcomes in this demonstration, ranging from 10 heads (and thus zero tails) to zero heads (and thus 10 tails). The laws of probability tell us how often you'll get 10 heads in 10 flips of a fair coin, 6 heads in 10 flips, 2 heads in 10 flips, and so forth. Excel has a function that tells you what those frequencies are: Excel supplies the logic, and you supply the specifics.

The function is BINOM.DIST, and the function's syntax is as follows:

```
BINOM.DIST(number_s,trials,probability_s,cumulative)
```

where:

- `number_s` is the number of successes: here, the number of times the coin comes up heads
- `trials` is the number of instances: here, the number of flips, or 10
- `probability_s` is the underlying probability of success: here, with a fair coin, that's 50%
- `cumulative`, if FALSE, tells Excel to return the probability of the associated number of heads only. If TRUE, it embraces all the probabilities of smaller numbers of successes, plus the current instance. So, if `cumulative` is TRUE, `BINOM.DIST` returns the cumulative probability of three heads as that of zero heads plus that of one head plus that of two heads plus that of three heads.

Notice in Figure 2.1 that cell E5 contains this formula:

```
=BINOM.DIST(B5,$B$1,$B$2,$B$3)
```

So:

- The number of successes—that is, the number of heads—is in cell B5
- The trials (here, the number of flips) is in cell $B$1
- The probability of getting heads on any given flip of the coin is in cell $B$2
- The value that determines whether to return the cumulative probability is in cell $B$3

Cell B5 is shown with a relative address so that when you copy from E5 into the range E6:E15, the address B5 will adjust its row accordingly, from 5 to 6, from 6 to 7, and so on. Cells B1 through B3 are shown with absolute addressing so that the addresses will not change as the formula is copied and pasted into E6:E15.

In Figure 2.2, notice that cell B3 contains FALSE, and therefore cells C8:C18 do *not* show cumulative probabilities but instead show the probability associated with each outcome.

Figure 2.2
BINOM.DIST's fourth, cumulative argument is not optional but required.

	D8	▾	⋮	✕	✓	*fx*	=SUM($C$8:$C8)		

⊿	A	B	C	D
1	Number of flips	10		
2	Coin's probability of Heads	50%		
3	Cumulative probability	FALSE		
4				
5			Probability	
6	Distribution of 10 flips		of number	Cumulative
7	Heads	Probability of:	of heads	probability
8	10	10 heads in 10 flips:	0.10%	0.10%
9	9	9 heads in 10 flips:	0.98%	1.07%
10	8	8 heads in 10 flips:	4.39%	5.47%
11	7	7 heads in 10 flips:	11.72%	17.19%
12	6	6 heads in 10 flips:	20.51%	37.70%
13	5	5 heads in 10 flips:	24.61%	62.30%
14	4	4 heads in 10 flips:	20.51%	82.81%
15	3	3 heads in 10 flips:	11.72%	94.53%
16	2	2 heads in 10 flips:	4.39%	98.93%
17	1	1 heads in 10 flips:	0.98%	99.90%
18	0	0 heads in 10 flips:	0.10%	100.00%
19				

Figure 2.3
The cumulative probabilities are more useful when they're charted.

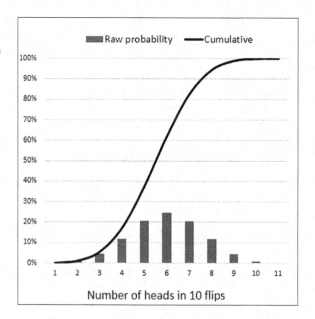

For example, in Figure 2.2, cell D9 shows the value 1.07. Allowing for a small amount of rounding error due to the display format, that value is the total of the values in cells C8:C9 in Figure 2.2. That is, it's a cumulative probability for the zero-heads instance of 0.1% and the one-heads instance of 0.98%.

Keep in mind that the results discussed in this section are *not* determined solely by coin flips. You would get the same results by pulling a card at random from a new deck and scoring a win if it's from a black suit and a loss if it's from a red suit. In each case there are two possible outcomes, a heads or a tails, a black card or a red card. There are 11 possible combinations: ten of red and zero of black, nine of red and one of black,..., zero of red and ten of black. Each combination has a particular long-term expected probability.

It is the latter probability that BINOM.DIST returns: in Figure 2.2, that's 4.39% in cell C10 for eight heads in ten flips (and also in cell C16, because this is a symmetric distribution—so, the probability of eight heads in ten is the same as the probability of two heads in ten). BINOM.DIST does not ask you how many sets of ten flips each you want to simulate. That's because its results are long-term expectations. You might repeat your ten flips hundreds of times without getting exactly 4.39% overall for eight out of ten, but you'll start to get very close once the total number of sets, of perhaps ten flips each, gets large enough to achieve a stable outcome.

For a meaningful number of reasons it's useful to know the *cumulative* percentage of successes: for example, the percentage of flips with zero heads, plus the percentage of flips with one head, with two heads, and so on. You can get the cumulative probability by setting BINOM.DIST's fourth argument to TRUE. You can also use a running total. If you have the raw percentages on the worksheet, as in cells C8:C18 in Figure 2.2, then you might add this formula in D8:

```
=SUM($C$8:$C8)
```

and drag it down through D9:D18. Figure 2.3 shows the results in charted form, with the raw percentages in the Column format and the cumulative percentages in the Line format.

Understanding Some Related Functions

Excel has some functions that are closely related to BINOM.DIST. I'll mention them here, even though the concepts I've discussed in this chapter have largely the same effect as they do when used with those other functions.

Excel offers a function named BINOM.INV, which returns the inverse of the BINOM.DIST function. BINOM.INV is useful in acceptance sampling, helping both a buyer and a seller decide whether a full lot of goods falls below a negotiated criterion for percentage of defects. Compare the syntax of these two Excel functions:

```
BINOM.DIST(number_s,trials,probability_s,cumulative)
BINOM.INV(trials,probability_s,alpha)
```

If you compare the argument list for BINOM.DIST to that for BINOM.INV, you'll notice that:

■ You need to supply both functions with the number of trials (trials) and the long-term probability of the event (probability_s). In the example that this chapter has discussed, *trials* is 10 coin flips and *probability_s* is 0.5 or 50% because our assumption has been that you're using a fair coin.

■ You also need to supply the cumulative argument to BINOM.DIST.

■ The main differences between the two functions are as follows:

• You supply number_s to BINOM.DIST—that's the number of *successes* in trials—and it returns alpha, the probability associated with number_s, given the other arguments.

• You supply alpha to BINOM.INV and it returns number_s, again given the other arguments.

So:

```
=BINOM.DIST(4, 10, 0.5, FALSE)
```

returns **0.2051**, and

```
=BINOM.INV(10, 0.5, 0.2051)
```

returns **4**.

You'll find that functions that deal with several other distributions, including the beta, gamma, chi squared, *t*, *F*, log-normal and normal, have similar distinctions between their DIST and INV forms in Excel.

> **NOTE** It makes sense that you would need to specify a *cumulative* argument for the `BINOM.DIST` function, because you might want either the probability of a particular number of successes (set *cumulative* to FALSE) *or* the sum of the probabilities for a range of successes (set *cumulative* to TRUE). It does not make sense that you would want a cumulative total of the numbers of successes—at least, not in the context of a probability analysis. There are much easier ways in Excel to find the total of consecutive integers, such as $= 1 + 2 + 3 + 4$.

You also might notice that Excel offers a `BINOMDIST` function (note the absence of the period in the function name) and a `CRITBINOM` function. These are legacy functions from early versions of Excel. The Help documentation states that the current versions might be more accurate than the functions' legacy counterparts.

Let's take a closer look at the results in C8:C18 in Figure 2.2. Cell C14 shows that the probability of getting four heads in ten flips of a fair coin is 20.51%. Suppose that you tried out this example in reality and got 20.51% for five heads in ten flips and 24.61% for four flips of ten. That's the reverse of what you expect: with a fair coin, you expect four heads in 20.51% of ten flips and five heads in 24.61% of ten flips (see cells C13:C14).

Does that mean that you don't really have a fair coin? That the long-run average for heads with this coin is less than 24.61%?

Most reasonable people would disagree with that. For them, the evidence simply wouldn't be strong enough to reject the hypothesis that it's a fair, 50% coin. Both intuitively and mathematically, you *expect* to get three, four, six, or seven tails in 64.45% of ten-flip tests. You'd likely be more comfortable chalking up the extra tails flips (or the extra heads flips) to random chance than to suspect the coin of being a ringer.

But you might reach a different conclusion. What if your trial results favored not four or five heads in ten flips but three heads in ten? A fair coin will behave that way only 11.72% of the time (see cell C15 in Figure 2.2). To you, that might make a difference. A result that's two flips away from a fair coin's long-term expectation might be good enough for you to suspect that someone had laid hands on a counterfeit coin.

You might decide that a difference of two flips out of ten, three heads instead of five heads in ten flips, is plenty big enough to make you doubt the coin's fairness. If you prefer to think in terms of percentages rather than raw numbers, you might decide that a difference of 12.89% (that is, 24.61% less 11.72%) deserves closer attention than 4.10% (that is, 24.61% less 20.51%).

If there were something at issue more consequential than a coin flip—for example, whether a vaccine is safe or toxic—then you would doubtless want to buttress the evidence with related empirical research and cost/benefit analyses. But at root, the decision is subjective and rests on how you regard the costs of a bad choice in light of the benefits of a good one. I'll return to this issue later when we look at A/B tests in Bayesian analysis.

But first it's necessary to show how to run binomial tests in R rather than in Excel. That will ease the subsequent transitions when we reach the point of quadratic approximations and Markov Chain Monte Carlo (MCMC).

Working with R's Binomial Functions

For consistency with functions that work with distributions other than the binomial, R tends to build more functionality into its binomial analyses more finely than does Excel. Recall that Excel has two primary binomial functions: BINOM.DIST, which returns the probability associated with different numbers of successes, and BINOM.INV, which returns the number of successes associated with different probabilities.

In contrast, R offers these binomial functions:

- dbinom(x, size, prob, log = FALSE)—R's version of BINOM.DIST. The "d" in dbinom stands for "density." The first, or x, argument to dbinom can be a single value; then, dbinom returns the probability of successes associated with that grouping—say, four heads of ten flips. If x is instead a vector, as shown in the next section, then dbinom returns a vector of probabilities, each associated with a value in x.

- pbinom(q, size, prob, lower.tail = TRUE, log.p = FALSE)—R's version of BINOM. DIST, but the probabilities returned are cumulative sums. Whereas BINOM.DIST might return 3%, 4%, and 5% as the probabilities of Event 1, Event 2, and Event 3, pbinom might return 3%, 7%, and 12%, respectively. In contrast, Excel relies on you to use worksheet functions to convert BINOM.DIST's event-specific probabilities to cumulative sums of probabilities. BINOM.DIST's cumulative argument is not optional. pbinom has a lower.tail argument that enables you to accumulate from the top down instead of from the bottom up.

- qbinom(p, size, prob, lower.tail = TRUE, log.p = FALSE)—R's version of BINOM. INV. You supply p, a probability or vector of probabilities. That is qbinom's first argument. You also supply size (the number of trials, such as ten flips) and prob (the probability of an event, here .5 for a heads). R returns the cumulative number of successes such as [0, 1, 2] and so on, associated with the success rate represented by each quantile. (Yes, this is confusing. I discuss it further in later sections of this chapter.)

- rbinom(n, size, prob)—Excel has no built-in version of this function. It returns random values from a binomial distribution.

Using R's dbinom Function

To use dbinom effectively, you must be able to prepare and pass a vector of values to the dbinom function. Each value represents some number of successes: that is, zero heads in ten flips, one head in ten flips, and so on. The dbinom function uses this vector, in conjunction with two more arguments, to return the probability associated with each number of successes.

For example, enter this command in R's console, just right of the > command prompt:

```
successes = seq(0, 10, by = 1)
```

That command establishes the vector of the number of successes or flips that result in a heads. R responds by showing another command prompt on the next blank line in the console. Enter this command to see the vector you just created:

```
successes
```

R responds with the contents of the vector `successes`:

```
[1]  0  1  2  3  4  5  6  7  8  9 10
```

In this case, the `seq` function created the vector with eleven values, because it starts with zero as its first value and ends at 10. The number in square brackets at the left end of the output indicates the index of the value in the vector immediately to its right. So, if R had room for only five values in the first row of the output, the second line would begin with [6]. If you're displaying the output in the R console rather than writing it to a file, the room that R has available is dictated by the width of the console as you've set it on the screen.

Now, enter this command in the console:

```
probabilities=dbinom(successes,size=10,.5)
```

This command passes the contents of the vector `successes` to the `dbinom` function's first argument. The `size` argument is set to 10 in the argument list: it sets the number of trials to 10—in our example, a trial is a coin flip, so ten trials or flips. And the third argument gives the long-term expectation that the probability of a flip of this coin returns heads is 0.5, or 50%.

You can return the probability of each number of heads (that is, the number of successes) by entering this command in the console:

```
probabilities
```

You'll get these results:

```
 [1] 0.0009765625
 [2] 0.0097656250
 [3] 0.0439453125
 [4] 0.1171875000
 [5] 0.2050781250
 [6] 0.2460937500
 [7] 0.2050781250
 [8] 0.1171875000
 [9] 0.0439453125
[10] 0.0097656250
[11] 0.0009765625
```

If you copy and paste these figures from the console and into an Excel worksheet, you can compare them with the results of the BINOM.DIST function that we looked at earlier in this chapter.

> **TIP** You will probably find it convenient to use Excel's Text-to-Columns command (on the Ribbon's Data tab) to remove the bracketed indices and convert the text format used on R's console to a Percent format provided by Excel.

If you have followed the instructions given in this chapter closely, you will see that R's dbinom function returns the same probabilities for different indices as does Excel's BINOM.DIST function.

> **NOTE** You might find it easier to use R's write.csv function to send the results of the dbinom function to a CSV file, and open that in Excel. This avoids the problems associated with converting R's text output to percentage values in Excel.

R's dbinom function also recognizes a log argument. By default, its value is FALSE. So, both these versions return 0.2051, the actual long-term percentage:

```
dbinom(4, 10, .5, log = FALSE)
dbinom(4, 10, .5)
```

If you set it to TRUE, the function returns –1.584364:

```
dbinom(4, 10, .5, log = TRUE)
```

Using R's pbinom **Function**

If you use the same arguments as above but with pbinom rather than dbinom, you get cumulative probabilities. If you establish a vector named successes, as in the previous section, then this function:

```
pbinom(successes,10,.5)
```

returns this vector:

```
 [1] 0.0009765625
 [2] 0.0107421875
 [3] 0.0546875000
 [4] 0.1718750000
 [5] 0.3769531250
 [6] 0.6230468750
 [7] 0.8281250000
 [8] 0.9453125000
 [9] 0.9892578125
[10] 0.9990234375
[11] 1.0000000000
```

Note that if you keep a running total of the values returned by dbinom, you get the values returned by pbinom.

Cumulative probabilities are important in the field of acceptance sampling, where you often want to know the probability of one defective unit, plus the probability of two such units, plus the probability of three, and so on through the limit of the trials. Earlier in this chapter I noted that `pbinom` takes an argument called `lower.tail`. Here's the rationale. Conventionally, the first argument to both `dbinom` and `pbinom` is termed, and thought of, as the number of *successful trials*—for example, only three heads out of ten flips.

But when you're interested in the number of *failed trials* in a production lot, you're therefore also interested not in the cumulative instances of 1, 2, 3, etc. successes, but in the cumulative instances of 10, 9, 8, etc. failures.

Visualize the vector of probabilities returned by `pbinom`. In the normal state of affairs, you're interested in counts of successes, and you start accumulating the probabilities with the count of instances at zero successes and end (perhaps, as in our example) at ten. You start accumulating at the lower end of the distribution, and the `lower.tail` argument is (and defaults to) TRUE.

But when you're interested in the failures, it's convenient to accumulate counts of failures, and you accomplish that by changing the value of `lower.tail` to FALSE from its default value of TRUE. Then, the accumulation begins at the upper end rather than the lower end of the distribution.

And there's one more argument to `pbinom`, `log.p`. Setting it to TRUE causes `pbinom` to return the log of the probabilities rather than the raw values, so that they can be added rather than multiplied—among other conveniences.

Using R's `qbinom` Function

The `qbinom` function uses this syntax:

```
qbinom(p, size, prob, lower.tail = TRUE, log.p = FALSE)
```

Its equivalent in Excel is

```
=BINOM.INV(size, prob, p)
```

where

- `p` is the probability associated with a given number of successes (for example, the probability of scoring eight heads in ten flips)
- `size` is the number of trials (for example, the number of coin flips in one set of flips)
- `prob` is the probability inherent in the event (for example, 0.5 for the flip of a fair coin)

Figure 2.4 illustrates the relationship between the number of defective items found in a sample of 100 items and the percent defective to be expected in a full lot of the items.

Figure 2.4
The result of R's qbinom function is interpreted by Excel documentation as the smallest value larger than a criterion. Here the criterion could be the maximum number of defects in a sample before the entire lot is rejected.

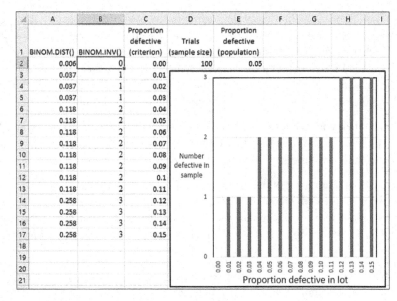

	A	B	C	D	E	F	G	H	I
			Proportion defective (criterion)	Trials (sample size)	Proportion defective (population)				
1	BINOM.DIST()	BINOM.INV()							
2	0.006	0	0.00	100	0.05				
3	0.037	1	0.01						
4	0.037	1	0.02						
5	0.037	1	0.03						
6	0.118	2	0.04						
7	0.118	2	0.05						
8	0.118	2	0.06						
9	0.118	2	0.07						
10	0.118	2	0.08						
11	0.118	2	0.09						
12	0.118	2	0.1						
13	0.118	2	0.11						
14	0.258	3	0.12						
15	0.258	3	0.13						
16	0.258	3	0.14						
17	0.258	3	0.15						
18									
19									
20									
21									

The vertical axis in Figure 2.4 represents the number of defective items found in the sample. The horizontal axis represents the proportion of items in the full lot that you can expect to be defective. Again, this sort of analysis is more frequently seen in acceptance sampling than other procedures. Let's have a look at how that might work.

Using R and qbinom in Quality Testing

I want to explore the topic of acceptance sampling and the qbinom function in more detail here because many people, myself included, find its logic a little circuitous at first. Looking at the function and its results from outside the Bayesian framework can help clarify that logic.

Consider this situation: You have negotiated the purchase of a complex piece of machinery to be installed in your own product as part of the final assembly process. The company that will manufacture the component for you has a reputation for quality merchandise, but this will be its first experience making the component in question. The principals agree that you may return the first shipment as defective if, using conventional acceptance sampling tools, you find that the first shipment of 100 units contains 5% or more that are defective.

Those tools mean that you will draw a unit at random from the shipment and test it. You'll repeat that process until the maximum acceptable number of defectives is reached. At that point, if it comes about, testing stops. You don't want to test all 100 units if you don't have to because it's a time-consuming, expensive process. Furthermore, you're in the business of assembling end-user products, not shipping a carton of 100 units back to their manufacturer because one unit too many was defective.

Using qbinom

How do you know if you have reached that testing criterion and should stop testing? You could test the entire shipment, but that can cost time and money, and is self-defeating if you must use destructive testing. Instead, use R and qbinom, or use Excel and BINOM.INV. Establish the boundaries of the probabilities in R using this code:

```
> p = seq(0, .15, by = .01)
```

You can see the contents of the vector simply by entering its name:

```
> p
 [1] 0.00 0.01 0.02 0.03 0.04 0.05 0.06 0.07
 [9] 0.08 0.09 0.10 0.11 0.12 0.13 0.14 0.15
```

Then run these commands in R:

```
> size = 100

> prob = .05
> qbinom(p,size,prob)
```

Using the syntax in R's documentation helps make the R code more self-documenting, but of course you could employ this command if you'd rather use the actual numbers for *size* (that is, the number of components sampled) and *prob* (that is, the hypothetical probability that will cause you to return the shipment to its manufacturer):

```
> qbinom(p,100,.05)
```

And R responds with these results:

```
[1] 0 1 1 1 2 2 2 2 2 2 2 2 3 3 3 3
```

These are the values of the binomial distribution that are associated with the probabilities you stored in the vector named *p*. As you'll see in the next section, in Figure 2.4, Excel returns the same results via its BINOM.INV function.

Using Excel and BINOM.INV in Quality Testing

In Figure 2.4, notice that the second through fourth values returned by BINOM.INV in B3:B5 each equal 1, and the fifth in B6 equals 2. That means that if you observe even one defective unit in the first four you test, you can conclude that the full lot has at least 5% defective units.

If you proceed to test the fifth unit, the rejection criterion increases from one to two. The criterion remains at two until the result of BINOM.DIST reaches 0.258 in cell A14. The rationale is that when the result of BINOM.DIST in column A is greater than the criterion in column C, the normal, expected proportion of defective units is greater than the comparison in column C. In the third row, for example, 0.037 in column A is greater than the 0.01 in column C. In that case, the criterion in column B does not change (here, from B3 to B4).

But in row 5, the 0.037 in A5 is greater than the comparison value 0.03 in C5, and so the criterion value in column B increments, from B5 to B6.

It's important to realize that the value returned by both `BINOM.INV` and `qbinom` depends on three numbers: the sample size (Excel calls this *trials*; R calls it *size*), the hypothesized proportion of successes (Excel calls this *probability_s*; R calls it *prob*), and the vector of probabilities that represent your range of interest (Excel calls this *alpha*; R calls it *p*).

Here are the steps to run the analysis in Excel. Enter this sequence in, say, C2:C17:

0.00, 0.01, 0.02 ... 0.15

This is the same vector that you assigned to the variable *p* in the previous section.

In Excel, you can get the same results as using `qbinom`, with this formula entered in cell B2:

`=BINOM.INV($D$2,$E$2, C2)`

Copy and paste it down into B3:B17. It assumes that the number 100 is in cell D2 and the number 0.05 in cell E2. Notice that the results of the `BINOM.INV` function are the same as those returned by `qbinom` in the previous section.

To reconcile the arguments as they're used in this example:

- R's documentation refers to the number of components to test as *size*. Excel's documentation uses the term *trials*. In this example, its value is 100.
- R's documentation refers to the value that you're testing for as *prob*. Excel's term is *probability_s*. In this example, its value is 0.05.
- R's documentation refers to the vector of probabilities as *p*. Excel's term is *alpha*. In this example, it's a vector held in R's memory, and in Excel the same sequence of decimal fractions might be in C2:C17, as in Figure 2.4.

Using R's `rbinom` Function

You can use R's `rbinom` function to establish a vector of random values based on a binomial distribution. You need to supply a specific number of random values (n), the number of instances of trials in each set (size), and the success probability of an individual trial (prob), leading to this syntax:

`rbinom(n, size, prob)`

The `rbinom` function is useful when you are establishing priors by means of more complex methods than those that use a simple binomial distribution.

Grappling with the Math

To this point, this book has discussed the distribution of values of variables that are usually described as "nominal" or "categorical." The principal issue to bear in mind is that categories have firm boundaries. The quantity of defective items in a sample is a good example: If a sample contains five defective items, two of those items might contain one or more true defects and one item with defects that don't matter very much. You still have three defective items, not two-and-a-quarter defective items. If you have a carton of items with defects, it might contain 12 items. The carton won't be thought of as containing 11 truly defective items and an item that's only half defective. (But a branch of acceptance sampling does concern itself with types of defects, some of which might be cause for rejection and some not.)

Continuous variables are another story entirely. A continuous variable can have a distribution with values, and those values can have frequencies of occurrence and therefore percentages of occurrence. Temperature, height, and cholesterol level are continuous variables. Seventy-two and a half inches is a perfectly acceptable value for human height. Seventy-two and a half defective items is not an acceptable value for a count of defects in a production lot: that half-a-defect spoils the count. One item with a partial defect counts as a defective item, not half a defective item.

Although this distinction restricts the range within which categorical variables are appropriate for analysis, the distinction makes them easier to analyze. The frequency of items in a category is merely a count of its items. To get its probability of occurrence, just divide the category count by the size of the full sample.

Matters are different with continuous variables. Figure 2.5 shows the distribution of a normal curve, from –1.0 to +1.0 z-scores.

Figure 2.5
Somewhere along the line, calculus must come into play in the analysis of the distribution of a continuous variable.

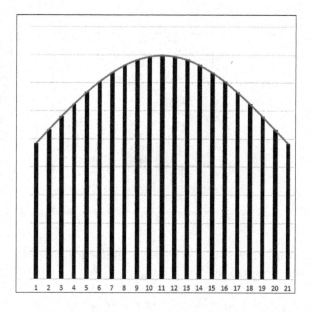

If each column represented the frequency of occurrence of a value in a categorical variable, the line between the top of each column and an adjacent one would be straight, and the count of each category would be exactly proportional to the column's height plus the triangular area at its top.

But if Figure 2.5 represents a continuous variable, then the line between the tops of adjacent columns is an arc, not a straight line. That amount of curvature in a segment of that line depends on its location along the range of the values of the continuous variable, as well as on the distance between columns. To get an accurate estimate of the proportion or frequency of cases anywhere along the distribution of a continuous variable, we need to apply integral calculus. Fortunately, that calculus is hidden inside functions that are analogous to the `BINOM` functions in Excel and the `binom` functions in R. I'll explore that issue in greater detail (without resorting to an integral symbol or a differential) when we take up the beta distribution in Chapter 8.

In the meantime, nominal variables enable us to avoid calculus entirely, whether hidden inside other functions or not. It's occasionally useful to be able to calculate the binomial distribution without resorting to R's `dbinom` or Excel's `BINOM.DIST` function. ("That's a ridiculous figure I'm getting from `BINOM.DIST`; I'd better take it apart and see what's going on.") Figure 2.6 shows how that's done, without resorting to anything more complicated than an exponent.

Figure 2.6
The "nCr" calculation is at the heart of the binomial distribution.

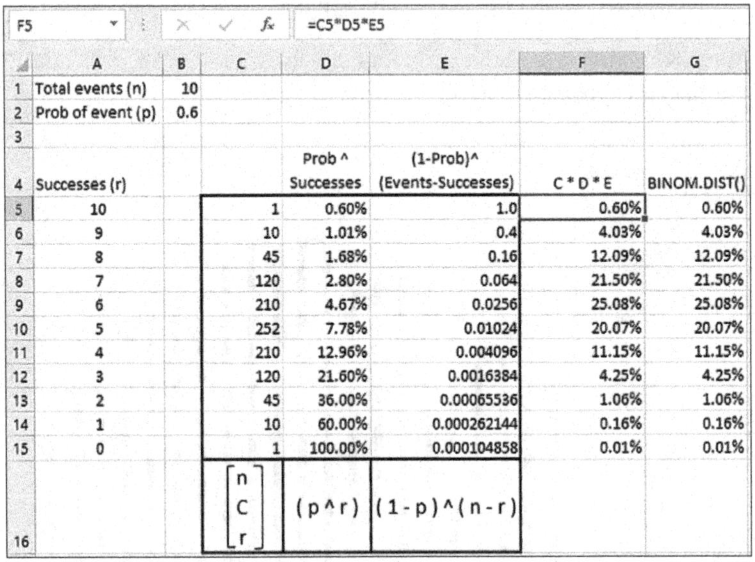

F5 =C5*D5*E5

	A	B	C	D	E	F	G
1	Total events (n)	10					
2	Prob of event (p)	0.6					
3							
4	Successes (r)			Prob ^ Successes	(1-Prob)^ (Events-Successes)	C*D*E	BINOM.DIST()
5	10		1	0.60%	1.0	0.60%	0.60%
6	9		10	1.01%	0.4	4.03%	4.03%
7	8		45	1.68%	0.16	12.09%	12.09%
8	7		120	2.80%	0.064	21.50%	21.50%
9	6		210	4.67%	0.0256	25.08%	25.08%
10	5		252	7.78%	0.01024	20.07%	20.07%
11	4		210	12.96%	0.004096	11.15%	11.15%
12	3		120	21.60%	0.0016384	4.25%	4.25%
13	2		45	36.00%	0.00065536	1.06%	1.06%
14	1		10	60.00%	0.000262144	0.16%	0.16%
15	0		1	100.00%	0.000104858	0.01%	0.01%
16			nCr	(p^r)	(1-p)^(n-r)		

The "nCr" formula is usually spoken as "n things taken r at a time, or as "n choose r." It returns the number of ways to combine n things into groups of size r. So, three people—Alice, Bob, and Carol—can be paired up in three ways: Alice and Bob, Bob and Carol, Alice and Carol. You can get that count using the nCr formula:

nCr = n! / ((n – r)! r!)

where we want to know the number of combinations of size *r* that can be made of *n* elements. The exclamation point in that formula means *factorial*, by the way. The expression 4! means 4 × 3 × 2 × 1. (The exclamation point is usually pronounced "bang," as in "four bang.")

So, with three elements and groups of size 2, we have:

3! / ((3 − 2)! × 2!

or 6 / (1 × 2), or 3. That's not yet what we're after, though. As Figure 2.6 shows, we have to put three more quantities into the picture:

- p, the probability of a given event. If you're working with coin flips, the probability of getting a named side of the coin is 0.5; if a deck of cards, 1/52; if a six-sided die, it's 16.67%. On Figure 2.6, p is in cell B2.

- n, the number of events, in cell B1. Suppose that you want to assess whether a coin is fair. You decide that an experiment with the coin will consist of ten flips, after which you will record the number of times the coin comes up heads. You repeat the experiment with another ten flips, and yet again. The number of events is ten—ten flips of the coin.

- r, the number of successful events. If you flip a coin ten times and get six heads, r equals 6.

Summary

Let's move on to the beta distribution. As you'll see, the beta has both crucial similarities and crucial differences vis-à-vis the binomial. The binomial, as you've seen in this chapter, is characterized by what tend to be naturally occurring boundaries between a variable's values.

A beta distribution does not have boundaries of that sort: it is continuous rather than discrete. This aspect of a beta distribution has implications for the functions that you choose (pbeta instead of pbinom, for example) as well as the inferences that you can draw from their use. You'll find that most of the capabilities that you can find in the binomial family are replicated, bearing in mind the differences between the two types of distribution, in the beta family.

Understanding the Beta Distribution

3

The previous chapter discussed the binomial distribution and how to use Excel's worksheet functions, as well as R's family of binomial functions, to explore the inferences that you can make from those functions.

This chapter explores some of the reasons why you might decide to use a distribution other than the binomial distribution as your point of reference. That's the *beta distribution*.

In a variety of ways, the beta distribution resembles the binomial. For example, both distributions lend themselves well to the analysis of events that can take on one of two values, such as heads or tails, true or false, survives or fails to survive. One consequence of analyzing that sort of event is that you wind up with discrete categories—categories that you can easily count.

For example, you might want to analyze the fairness of a coin—that is, whether the coin is as likely to come up heads as it is to come up tails. Simply as a consequence of the way that the event is measured, you inevitably wind up with outcome categories, such as zero heads in ten flips, one head in ten flips, two heads, and so on. It's unusual even to take account of a flipped coin landing and staying on its edge, so your categories would not include five and a half heads in ten flips.

And yet, if you were recording LDL cholesterol measures instead of coin flips, you would want to record them with as fine-grained a metric as possible, in order to take advantage of the fact that your measuring instrument is much more sensitive than a coin. You expect to learn more if you can record and study a record that measures a subject's LDL as *80.55* rather than *between 80 and 85*.

But so fine-grained a metric isn't of much use if your software can't handle it. While the binomial distribution usually can't, the beta distribution can, and this chapter goes about the business of explaining how.

Establishing the Beta Distribution in Excel

Let's start, as the prior chapter did, by inventorying the pertinent worksheet functions in Excel.

> **NOTE** I make that suggestion because it's hard to find a computer that doesn't have Excel installed, and because so many users got their first taste of discrete distributions using Excel's functions. Familiarity breeds confidence.

Just two functions in Excel have to do with the binomial distribution (setting aside legacy functions): BINOM.DIST, which returns information about the area under the distribution's curve, and BINOM.INV, which returns information about the categories that comprise the curve.

The pattern that Excel uses for the beta distribution is similar. Excel offers a BETA.DIST function, which returns an area associated with a quantile, and a BETA.INV function, which returns information about the quantile associated with an area.

> **NOTE** A quantile is a point along a scale that divides a probability—such as an area under a curve—into equal quantities. Familiar quantiles include percentiles and quartiles. Assuming that the values are sorted in ascending order, the first percentile is the point on a scale below which you find the lowest 1% of the values. The second percentile captures an additional 1% of the values. The first quartile separates the lower 25% of the values from the upper 75%. The median divides the area into two 50% halves.

BETA.DIST and BETA.INV are inverses of one another, in a manner that's similar to how BINOM.DIST and BINOM.INV are inverses of one another. So, to illustrate, consider this formula:

```
=BETA.DIST(0.47,18,31,TRUE)
```

which specifies the quantile in question at 0.47 (that is, 47%), the number of observed successes for that event at 18, and the number of observed failures at 31, and requests the total of all probabilities from quantiles of 0.0 to 0.47 (that is, the function's fourth, *cumulative* argument is TRUE). The function's result is 0.9292. The cumulative probability of 0 to 14 successful events is 92.9%.

Now consider the inverse of the previous formula:

```
=BETA.INV(0.9292,18,31)
```

which supplies as arguments to the BETA.INV function the cumulative probability of 0.9292 and the number of successes and failures (18 and 31). It returns 0.47. So the relationship between BETA.DIST and BETA.INV is inverse. You supply a quantile to BETA.DIST and it returns the associated probability. You supply a probability to BETA.INV and it returns the associated quantile.

Despite the close relationship between the BETA.DIST and the BETA.INV functions, the analogy isn't perfect. BETA.INV does not take a *cumulative* argument. BETA.DIST does, and it is required: there's no default value for *cumulative* in BETA.DIST.

Furthermore, both the BETA.DIST and the BETA.INV functions take the number of successes (e.g., heads) and the number of failures (e.g., tails) as arguments. But both BINOM.DIST and BINOM.INV take the number of successes (e.g., heads) and the number of *trials* (e.g., heads plus tails) as arguments. It's hard to see how it makes a difference, and Microsoft could have chosen to use the same pair in each function if only for consistency, but it didn't and now you know.

Comparing the Beta Distribution with the Binomial Distribution

Perhaps the most salient distinction between the binomial and the beta distributions is the nature of the quantiles that divide the total area under the curve into sectors. In a binomial distribution the sectors are discrete and range in relative size from relatively large (quartiles segment the total area into fourths and the median—or 50th percentile—divides it in half) to relatively small (percentiles segment the total area into one-hundredths). A beta distribution, in contrast, can be established, in theory, by dividing an infinite number of quantiles so that they define an infinite number of segments.

That's bad news and it's good news. The good news about the beta distribution is that you can pinpoint exactly where in the distribution any given value falls, down to the most minute degree of accuracy that your measuring stick provides you. In contrast, the binomial distribution doesn't necessarily tell you the particular percentile that a given value belongs to.

For example, refer to Figure 2.4. There you can see that a sample with only one defective unit might belong to the 0.01, the 0.02, or the 0.03 quantile. You can use the beta distribution to pinpoint an event's quantile to whatever degree of accuracy you want. More accuracy isn't always necessary, of course, but it's good to have it available when it's needed.

The bad news—and it's really not so bad—about the continuous nature of the beta distribution's quantiles is that a little extra computing is needed. Let's have a look at some of the math behind each distribution. First, a review of what Chapter 2 has to say about how the binomial is calculated.

Two figures are particularly important in considering any probability distribution, whether binomial, beta, normal, Poisson, whatever: the probability density function (PDF) and the probability mass function (PMF).

As Figure 2.6 shows, the formula for the binomial distribution's PDF is

```
nCr * p ^ r * [(1 - p) ^ (n - r)]
```

where:

- *n* might be the number of times you flip a coin.
- *p* might be the probability of getting a heads.
- *r* might be the number of times you actually get a heads in *n* flips.
- *nCr* is the number of combinations of *n* events, taken *r* events at a time. Excel provides this with a convenient function: `=COMBIN(n,r)`.

So the first factor in the equation, `nCr`, determines the number of ways that *n* events can be combined into groups of events each of size *r*. For example, there are 1,330 ways to combine 21 coins into groups of three heads each: `=COMBIN(21,3)`. And the second and third factors in the equation, `p ^ r` and `[(1 - p) ^ (n - r)]`, determine the probability (p) of the occurrence of several events and the probability of the non-occurrence (1 - p) of the same number of events. Because it's assumed that the events are independent of one another, their joint probability is equal to their product. So, `p ^ 3 = p * p * p` and, for their probability of non-occurrence, `(1 - p) ^ 3 = (1 - p) * (1 - p) * (1 - p)`.

> **NOTE** Bear in mind that all the events in a given quantile have, by definition, the same probability of occurrence; therefore, the sets of coin flips that comprise the 0.3 quantile have the same probability of heads—that is, 30%.

Now compare the formula for the binomial distribution with the formula for the beta distribution's PDF, which is given here:

```
PDF = [p ^ (α - 1) * (1 - p) ^ (β - 1)] / beta(α, β)
```

I hate to do this to you but it can't be helped. I've put it off as long as possible, but at this point we have to face the fact that this sort of analysis has some serious terminological deficiencies. They won't get in your way when you want to analyze data, but they are roadblocks to understanding what's going on inside the black box. Just keep in mind that Excel and R take care of this sort of thing for you.

First: The PDF formula just given returns a beta distribution. It tells you the quantity of observations you can expect when your trial results fail to follow the long-term expectation perfectly—for example, how frequently you can expect twelve tosses of a fair coin to come up with four heads and eight tails instead of six of each.

Fair enough, but the beta distribution uses something called the *beta function*, which is the final part—that is, the denominator—of the formula for the PDF:

```
beta(α, β)
```

So not only is the distribution named beta, the function is named beta and one of its two arguments is named beta. The two arguments to the beta function, α and β, are as they appear in the PDF function's numerator. That is, α is the number of successes and β is the number of failures. If you were analyzing the rolls of a single six-sided die, you would expect it in the long run to come up three 1/6 (that is, α) of the time and some other value 5/6 (that is, β) of the time.

And what is the beta function? It uses the gamma function. Gamma is represented by the Greek letter Γ in this formula:

```
beta(α, β)= Γ(α) * Γ(β) / Γ(α + β)
```

The *binomial distribution's* PDF uses the nCr formula to determine the number of combinations of successes in a series of trials. The nCr formula does so by making use of simple factorials, but simple factorials are defined only for integers, whereas the hallmark of the *beta distribution* is that its quantiles can represent fractional quantities. The Γ function gets us past that hurdle. (The Γ function is part of Excel's toolkit in the form of the GAMMA function.)

Figure 3.1 shows that the raw number formula for the beta distribution's PDF is equivalent to Excel's BETA.DIST function.

Figure 3.1
It's a lot easier to use Excel's BETA.DIST function than to build the analysis from scratch.

	Quantiles	=BETA.DIST()		Numerator	Beta function	Beta PDF	PDF as percent
Wins	10						
Losses	7						
	0	0.00000		0.000000	0.00001	0.00000	0.00%
	0.1	0.00004		0.000000	0.00001	0.00004	0.00%
	0.2	0.01075		0.000000	0.00001	0.01075	0.11%
	0.3	0.18544		0.000002	0.00001	0.18544	1.85%
	0.4	0.97943		0.000012	0.00001	0.97943	9.79%
	0.5	2.44385		0.000031	0.00001	2.44385	24.44%
	0.6	3.30556		0.000041	0.00001	3.30556	33.06%
	0.7	2.35578		0.000029	0.00001	2.35578	23.56%
	0.8	0.68788		0.000009	0.00001	0.68788	6.88%
	0.9	0.03102		0.000000	0.00001	0.03102	0.31%
	1	0.00000		0.000000	0.00001	0.00000	0.00%

Formula bar: =BETA.DIST(@Quantiles,Wins,Losses,FALSE)

Figure 3.1 requires some explanation. The main point is that the beta distribution's PDF, as calculated by Excel's BETA.DIST function, returns precisely the same results as does the formula for the PDF. Compare the function's results shown in the range B5:B15 with those in F5 to F15: they are identical.

I have named some important cells in the worksheet shown in Figure 3.1 to make the function and the formula a little easier to follow. The names and their references are

- *Wins*: Cell B1. This gives one of two values in a binomial distribution. I have labeled it *Wins* but it could just as easily be *Survives* or *Defective*. The value in cell B1 in Figure 3.1 is 10.

- *Losses*: Cell B2. This gives another of two values in a binomial distribution. I have labeled it *Losses* but it could just as easily be *Fails to Survive* or *Acceptable*. The value in cell B2 in Figure 3.1 is 7.

- *Quantiles*: Range A5:A15. This range contains a series of quantiles, in this case each representing one tenth of the curve's range: here, 0.0 to 1.0. Other quantiles that you might see or use are quartiles, quintiles (somewhat rarely), and percentiles. The values in the range A5:A15 are 0, 0.1, 0.2, … , 0.9, 1.0.

- *Betadist*: Range B5:B15. This range contains Excel's principal function to return the PDF, BETA.DIST. There are 11 instances of the following function in B5:B15:

  ```
  = BETA.DIST(@Quantiles,Wins,Losses,FALSE)
  ```

- *Numerator*: Range D5:D15. The values in this range are analogous to those in the binomial distribution's PDF. The numerator values help quantify the count of cases at each possible point in the horizontal axis of the distribution—for the binomial distribution, those are finite and measurable values, such as rolling a 3 on a single, six-sided die; for the beta distribution, they are a theoretically infinite number of continuous values. There are 11 instances of the following function in D5:D15:

  ```
  =@Quantiles^(Wins-1)*(1-@Quantiles)^(Losses-1)
  ```

- *Beta_function*: Range E5:E15. The beta function is defined in the previous section. Its purpose in the ratio that returns the beta PDF is to help *normalize* the ratio: that is, to cause the individual probabilities to total to 1, or 100%. The beta function is a ratio of values for the gamma function (represented here as Γ), which applies the factorial calculation to complex numbers. Recall that the binomial PDF calculates the factorials of counts of events, which are integers and therefore discrete. There are 11 instances of just one formula for the beta function in this range:

  ```
  Γ( Wins ) * Γ( Losses ) / Γ( Wins + Losses )
  ```

- You will obtain the proportions shown in B5:B15 if, after dividing the numerator by the beta function, you divide the result by the number of quantiles, minus 1. You'll find that latter calculation in H5:H15 of Figure 3.1.

CASE STUDY: THE @ SIGN AND THE IMPLICIT INTERSECTION

Notice in Figure 3.1 that the values in B5:B15 are identical to those in F5:F15 (allowing for the differences between decimal versus percent formatting). The values in B5:B15 are calculated by means of Excel's `BETA.DIST` function: that is, a multiple selection is made, encompassing the range B5:B15, and the following formula is entered via Ctrl + Enter:

```
=BETA.DIST(@Quantiles,Wins,Losses,FALSE)
```

If you have been using the same version of Excel for quite some time, you might not have seen the @ operator as it's used in the previous function. You use that operator (here, @) to inform Excel that the following name or reference (here, Quantiles) intersects the function or formula that makes reference to it.

So in this case the range named Quantiles in A5:A15 occupies the same rows as does the function `BETA.DIST` in B5:B15. This enables Excel to use the first row of Quantiles as an argument in the first row of `BETA.DIST`, the second row of Quantiles as an argument in the second row of `BETA.DIST`, and so on from worksheet row 5 through worksheet row 15. This arrangement ensures that Excel will use the proper value in Quantiles with the proper row occupied by `BETA.DIST`.

At one time you didn't need to do anything special (other than lining up the ranges properly) to invoke this feature. Excel was expected to know what to do when ranges occupied the same rows or columns and one range made use of another. The feature was then termed the *implicit intersection*. However, other changes that Microsoft has made to Excel's formula language have necessitated bringing the @ out from behind the bushes and showing itself in the formula or function where it's used, just as is done in the previous function described in this sidebar.

Figure 3.2 retains the quantiles in A5:A15 shown in Figure 3.1 and repeats the results returned by Excel's `BETA.DIST` function in B5:B15. Those results are divided by 10 (to normalize) and formatted as percentages in D5:D15.

Figure 3.2
Arranging for the percentages returned by `BINOM.DIST` or `BETA.DIST` is termed normalizing the data.

D10 | fx | =B10/10

	A	B	C	D	E
1	Wins	10			
2	Losses	7			
3					
4	Quantiles	=BETA.DIST()		PDF as percent	
5	0	0.00000		0.00%	
6	0.1	0.00004		0.00%	
7	0.2	0.01075		0.11%	
8	0.3	0.18544		1.85%	
9	0.4	0.97943		9.79%	
10	0.5	2.44385		24.44%	
11	0.6	3.30556		33.06%	
12	0.7	2.35578		23.56%	
13	0.8	0.68788		6.88%	
14	0.9	0.03102		0.31%	
15	1	0.00000		0.00%	

Notice that when the values in B5:B15 are divided by 9.99975 and formatted as percents, they total to 100%. (The difference between 9.99975 and 10.0 is due to very small errors of rounding in the calculus computations.) This is a useful characteristic, because when we're talking about event probabilities and the events are mutually exclusive and exhaustive, we want their percentages of occurrence to total to 1 (equivalently, to 100%).

Excel's BINOM.DIST and BETA.DIST functions, and the dbinom and dbeta functions in R, maintain the relative sizes of the values in each quantile (see Figure 3.3).

Figure 3.3
The results in column D have been normalized.

⊿	A	B	C	D	E	F	G
1	Wins	10					
2	Losses	7					
3							
4	Quantiles	=BETA.DIST()		PDF as percent			
5	0	0.00000		0.00%			
6	0.25	0.05437		1.37%			
7	0.5	2.44385		61.62%			
8	0.75	1.46796		37.01%			
9	1	0.00000		0.00%			
10							
11							
12	Total:	3.96618		100.00%			

(D7 — fx =B7/SUM(B$5:B$9))

In Figure 3.3, notice that I have reduced the number of quantiles from 11 to 5, creating an inclusive range that shows both its lower and upper limits. The values returned by BETA.DIST in B5:B9 now total to 3.9662. If you divide the results of BETA.DIST in B5:B9 by that total, or by 4, you'll get the normalized results shown in D5:D9: results that once again total to 100%. Normalizing the results of BINOM.DIST or BETA.DIST is usually helpful because then you have a better understanding of what is meant by, say, "Scores between 40 and 50 were between the first and second quantiles," than when you don't know the proportion of values that are within that range.

On the topic of quantiles, keep in mind that it's usually helpful to chart the results of BETA.DIST and BINOM.DIST, if only to understand the nature of the distribution better. There's usually little cost involved in increasing the number of quantiles if all you need to do is tell your software to run its calculations on 100 instead of five quantiles. Figure 3.4 shows the same beta distribution as in Figure 3.3.

The chart in Figure 3.4 is suggestive but inaccurate. Compare it with the chart in Figure 3.5, which is based on 100 quantiles, so each quantile is one percent further into the distribution. The chart in Figure 3.5 presents a much more accurate picture than does the chart in Figure 3.4.

Figure 3.4
The chart can be misleading if it shows too few quantiles.

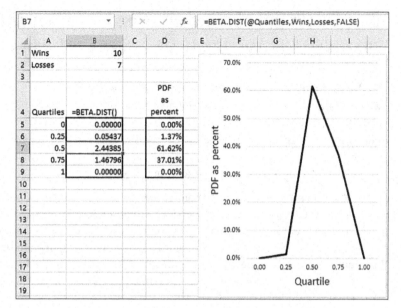

Figure 3.5
This chart is a much better depiction of what the beta distribution with 10 successes in 17 trials looks like.

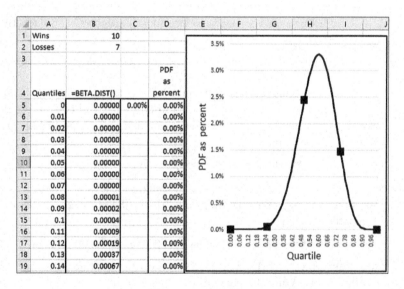

The chart in Figure 3.5 shows the 100 quantiles in column A as a curved line. It also shows the five quantiles from Figure 3.4 as individual squares that fall directly on the curve. If all you saw were the squares, your mind's eye might well fill in the missing data very differently.

Decoding Excel's Help Documentation for BETA.DIST

Here's what Excel's Help has to say about the second and third arguments to the BETA.DIST function:

- **Alpha:** Required. A parameter of the distribution.
- **Beta:** Required. A parameter of the distribution.

When I first read that, I couldn't tell what it was talking about. Granted that alpha and beta are parameters of the beta distribution, which ones are they? The mean and the variance? The median and the skewness? P-bar and theta? Now I ask you.

After some experimenting (and an unenlightening tour of Google) I figured out that alpha and beta are related to the mean, dispersion, and other descriptive measures, but only just barely. With the binomial distribution, we're still working with two values, A and Not-A, so True and False, Win and Loss, Sale and No Sale, but we supply number of trials rather than number of losses as the second argument to BINOM.DIST. In the beta distribution, *Alpha* refers to one of those values and *Beta* to the other, so it's 10 True and 7 False, or 10 Wins and 7 Losses, or 10 Sales and 7 No Sales.

> **NOTE** The mean of a beta distribution is $\alpha / (\alpha + \beta)$. Its variance is $\alpha\,\beta / [\,(\alpha + \beta)^2\,(\alpha + \beta + 1)]$.

Excel's A and B arguments (the fifth and sixth arguments to the BETA.DIST function) can also seem a little mysterious at first. They are optional, and you can use them to restrict the analysis to a subset of quantiles. For example, consider the analysis in Figure 3.5. The formulas in column B are

```
=BETA.DIST(@Quantiles,Wins,Losses,FALSE)
```

Notice that the A and B arguments are missing; in that case, they default to 0.0 and 1.0. To restrict the analysis to the quantiles from .01 to .10, use these formulas on the same rows as the quantiles of interest:

```
=BETA.DIST(@Quantiles,Wins,Losses,FALSE,0.01,0.10)
```

Excel returns the #NUM! error value whenever the associated quantile is outside the range bracketed by the A and B arguments (see Figure 3.6).

Figure 3.6
This analysis has been
deliberately limited to the
first few quantiles.

B6				f_x	=BETA.DIST(@Quantiles,Wins,Losses,FALSE,0.01,0.1)				

	A	B	C	D	E	F	G	H	I
1	Wins	10							
2	Losses	7							
3									
4	Quantiles	=BETA.DIST()							
5	0	#NUM!							
6	0.01	0.00000							
7	0.02	0.00113							
8	0.03	0.26032							
9	0.04	3.96865							
10	0.05	17.70125							
11	0.06	34.57275							
12	0.07	31.74919							
13	0.08	11.16108							
14	0.09	0.58003							
15	0.1	0.00000							
16	0.11	#NUM!							
17	0.12	#NUM!							

Replicating the Analysis in R

R has several functions that pertain to the beta distribution, analogous to those that pertain to the binomial distribution discussed in Chapter 2. The beta distribution functions in R include `dbeta`, `pbeta`, `qbeta`, and `rbeta`.

Using R, you can enter many statements directly in the Console window, where they are executed immediately. Sometimes, though, R will wait to do anything until you have finished a multi-line entry, such as a `For` loop. So, you might decide to enter your code in R's script window. From there, you can choose to execute your code one line at a time or the entire set of commands immediately.

To make that choice, take one of these steps:

- To execute one or more lines of code, click the line (or select the lines) in the script window and choose Edit, Run Line Or Selection.
- To execute all the lines of code in the script window, begin by making sure that the script window is active. (That's to ensure that the necessary commands are available in R's menu.) Then choose Run All. You needn't start by selecting the entire set of statements or the first statement in a block of code.

Understanding `dbeta`

The `dbeta` function returns the probability density function (PDF) for the quantile of a continuous variable. As such, it is analogous to the `dbinom` function, which is used with a discrete variable to return the probability mass function (PMF). The characteristic that most clearly distinguishes the PMF from the PDF is that it's necessary to use integration with a PDF to measure the difference in probability between two quantiles. Nothing more sophisticated than middle-school arithmetic is needed to quantify the difference in probability between two quantiles on a discrete scale.

The argument list for `dbeta` is similar to that for `dbinom`. From Chapter 2:

```
dbinom(x, size, prob, log = FALSE)
```

where *x* is a quantile such as 0.1666, distinguishable and discrete as a side on a six-sided die, *size* is some number of trials, *prob* is the theoretical probability for a single trial (say, 50% for a coin flip or 16.67% for the roll of a single die), and *log*, if FALSE or omitted, returns the resulting number of successes in *size* trials, or the log of that number if TRUE.

You could then enter the following commands into R's script window. When you start R, the console window appears. Choose File, New Script to display a fresh script window, and enter the following code there (see Figure 3.7).

Figure 3.7
Choose File, New Script to open a fresh R Editor window.

```
File  Edit  Format  View  Help
x <- seq( from = 0, to = 1, length.out = 101 )
Wins <- 10
Losses <- 7
density.out = dbeta( x , Wins , Losses )
write.csv(density.out, "beta_density.csv")
```

Click in the R Editor window to make sure it's active, and then choose Run All from R's Edit menu. The commands you typed will be repeated, along with any system messages, in the Console. If all goes well, a new file named beta_density.csv is written to your working directory. It contains the results of the `dbeta` functions. You can open a csv file using Excel (just double-click it), or you can use a text editor such as Notepad to open it.

The file is shown (with a chart added in Excel) in Figure 3.8.

Figure 3.8
I used Excel's Text To Columns command to convert R's output in the beta_density.csv file to figures that could be charted.

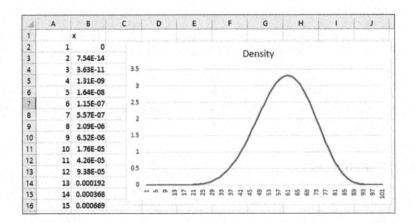

Understanding `pbeta`

You may recall from Chapter 2 that you can get the *cumulative* binomial distribution for a discrete variable by using the `pbinom` function. Let's revisit an example from Chapter 2. Begin by opening a fresh script window and entering into it these commands:

```
successes = seq(0, 10, by = 1)
probabilities = dbinom(successes, size=10,.5)
write.csv(probabilities,"dbinom_out.csv")
```

Then, choose Edit, Run All to execute those commands. A new csv file is written to your working directory.

Now edit your code in the script window so that it reads as follows (I've shown the two changes in boldface):

```
successes = seq(0, 10, by = 1)
probabilities = pbinom(successes, size=10,.5)
write.csv(probabilities,"pbinom_out.csv")
```

If you open the two csv files, dbinom_out.csv and pbinom_out.csv, you'll see what's shown in Figure 3.9. (I have combined the two result files into one worksheet to make it easier to compare them in one figure.) The results of using R's `dbinom` function are in the range B3:B13. They show the expected proportion of the trials that will have the same number of successes as the associated quantile in A3:A13. So, for example, you would expect that 0.2051 of the trials to have five occurrences of events with a 50% probability (Figure 3.9, A7:B7).

Figure 3.9
Differences between
`dbinom` and `pbinom`.

	A	B	C	D	E	F	G
1							Cumulative
2	x	dbinom()		x	pbinom()		on dbinom()
3	1	0.0010		1	0.0010		0.0010
4	2	0.0098		2	0.0107		0.0107
5	3	0.0439		3	0.0547		0.0547
6	4	0.1172		4	0.1719		0.1719
7	5	0.2051		5	0.3770		0.3770
8	6	0.2461		6	0.6230		0.6230
9	7	0.2051		7	0.8281		0.8281
10	8	0.1172		8	0.9453		0.9453
11	9	0.0439		9	0.9893		0.9893
12	10	0.0098		10	0.9990		0.9990
13	11	0.0010		11	1.0000		1.0000

The results of using R's `pbinom` function are in the range E3:E13. The values there are cumulative sums: in other words, the value 0.1719 in cell E6 is the sum of the first four quantiles, from x = 1 to x = 4 in B3:B6.

You can verify this easily enough by examining the cells in the range G3:G13 in Figure 3.9. There, the cumulative probability sums are obtained by adding the prior sum to the probability of the current quantile. So, the formula =G5+B6 in cell G6 is the prior sum in G5 plus the probability for quantile 4 in cell B6. You can save yourself the trouble of accumulating probability totals, as in column G, by using `pbinom` to begin with, before leaving R.

That said, you might use an analogous procedure—pbeta rather than pbinom—if you were working with a continuous variable instead of a discrete variable. Have a look at Figure 3.10.

Figure 3.10
To get a cumulative sum of probabilities using a continuous—not a discrete—variable, use integration instead of simple addition.

	A	B	C	D	E	F	G	H
1	Wins	10						
2	Losses	7						
3				Running sum				With
4		dbeta		cum dbeta		pbeta		integration
5	0	0.00000		0.00000		0.00000		0.00000
6	0.1	0.00000		0.00000		0.00000		0.00000
7	0.2	0.00107		0.00108		0.00025		0.00025
8	0.3	0.01854		0.01962		0.00713		0.00713
9	0.4	0.09794		0.11757		0.05832		0.05832
10	0.5	0.24438		0.36195		0.22725		0.22725
11	0.6	0.33056		0.69251		0.52717		0.52717
12	0.7	0.23558		0.92808		0.82469		0.82469
13	0.8	0.06879		0.99687		0.97334		0.97334
14	0.9	0.00310		0.99997		0.99950		0.99950
15	1	0.00000		0.99997		1.00000		1.00000

In Figure 3.10, the range B5:B15 shows the breakdown of the total probability of 17 events (ten successes and seven failures) according to R's dbeta function. The range D5:D15 contains the sum of the probabilities in previous quantiles plus the probability of the current quantile—sometimes termed a *running sum*. This is just how we calculated the cumulative probabilities for a discrete variable, using dbinom and pbinom in Figure 3.9.

The problem is that the running sums in D5:D15 don't match the results of pbeta in F5:F15. But the documentation says that pbeta returns the cumulative probability density values.

And so it does. What the running sum approach to accumulation omits is all those quantiles in between the ten used in the present example. Bear in mind that you can divide a continuous variable into a theoretically infinite number of values. Each quantile that we add to the analysis makes the running sum a little more accurate, but the arithmetic can never make it a perfectly accurate accumulation. There's always another quantile you can add to a continuum of an infinite number of values. It's a variation of Achilles Paradox.

The pbeta function in R is highly accurate (no calculus is perfectly accurate), and the running sum method starts as fairly inaccurate but becomes more accurate as more quantiles are added to the problem. To demonstrate this, you can run a simple set of statements in R, which I've used to calculate the values shown in H5:H15 of Figure 3.10. Note that they are identical to the values produced by pbeta in F5:F15. For the example in Figure 3.10, the code used is as follows:

```
p <- seq(0, 1, length=11)
for(i in 1:11) {
  x=integrate(function(p) dbeta(p, 10, 7),  0, p[i])
  print (x)
}
```

The code instructs R to calculate the integral that measures the area under the beta distribution's curve between zero and each quantile stored in p—that is, the quantiles 0.0, 0.1, 0.2, and so on. These areas are the total probability associated with events occurring between zero and each of the processed quantiles. After each integral is computed and stored temporarily in x, the integral is printed to R's console, along with an estimate of the (usually tiny) error associated with the calculation of each integral.

But it's easier to use pbeta.

Understanding qbeta

The qbeta function, like the corresponding qbinom function for discrete variables, returns a quantile when you supply a probability. For example, this command:

```
qbeta(.6, 10, 7)
```

returns a quantile of 0.622. In words: With alpha equal to 10 and beta equal to 7, a probability of 0.6 is associated with a quantile of 0.622 in the beta distribution.

You could try checking that by means of the dbeta function with 0.622 as the quantile:

```
dbeta(0.622,10,7)
```

but that returns a (normalized) value of 0.326, not the 0.6 that qbeta might have led you to expect. But keep in mind that while dbeta returns probabilities, they are point estimates rather than *cumulative* probabilities, and therefore not additive across quantiles. In contrast, if you entered the function for a cumulative probability:

```
pbeta(.622,10,7)
```

it would return 0.6 as expected. Figure 3.11 charts the PDF for the beta distribution with an alpha of 10 and a beta of 7. You can duplicate the results shown in Figure 3.11 by running the five lines of code shown in the prior section.

Figure 3.11

Notice that the raw probability exceeds the cumulative probability until the mean α / (α + β) of the distribution is reached.

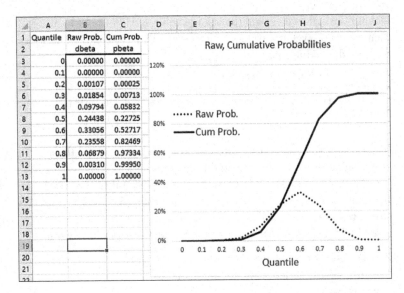

Quantile	Raw Prob. dbeta	Cum Prob. pbeta
0	0.00000	0.00000
0.1	0.00000	0.00000
0.2	0.00107	0.00025
0.3	0.01854	0.00713
0.4	0.09794	0.05832
0.5	0.24438	0.22725
0.6	0.33056	0.52717
0.7	0.23558	0.82469
0.8	0.06879	0.97334
0.9	0.00310	0.99950
1	0.00000	1.00000

About Confidence Intervals

It's about time to start discussing the use of Bayesian techniques on statistical problems. R's qbeta function is a good place to start because of its relationship to confidence intervals. A confidence interval is a subset of a scale that expresses both the variability of individual values and the location of a statistic (such as the mean) along that scale.

Frequentists and Bayesians have slightly different conceptions of the meaning of a confidence interval, and these differences are reflected in the use of alternative terms such as "credible interval" and "compatibility interval." I'll touch on those differences, rather briefly, in the remainder of this chapter.

The traditional, frequentist interpretation goes like this: You have a mean value of, say, systolic blood pressure measurements taken from a sample of actual observations. That sample also provides you with a standard deviation of those observations.

Of course, errors of various sorts get in your way. Sampling error, equipment malfunctions, poor procedure on the part of the people who take the readings, high anxiety experienced by the subjects, your own errors in transcribing the data—each of these contributes somehow to an erroneous estimate of the population's mean systolic pressure by way of the sample's mean systolic pressure.

So you decide to put a confidence interval around your sample mean. This interval is a segment of the systolic scale—say, from 115 to 125—within which may or may not be hidden the population mean, along with the sample mean. The population mean is unencumbered by the sources of random error to which your real-life sample is susceptible; their cumulative effect accounts for any difference that might exist between the sample mean and the population mean.

It would improve matters if you could get your hands on a *batch* of samples—say, 99 of them—each sample comprising subjects equivalent to those you've already sampled. You could calculate the mean of each sample and calculate the standard deviation of those means, a statistic called the *standard error of the mean*. Then, you could put the lower bracket of your confidence interval one standard error below your sample mean, and the upper bracket one standard error above your sample mean. If the standard error turned out to be five points on the systolic scale, your confidence interval would run from 115 (lower bracket) through 120 (sample mean) to 125 (upper bracket).

If you did all this, you'd wind up with a 68% confidence interval. Sixty-eight of the hypothetical confidence intervals would capture the population mean of 124. Why 68%? Because the distribution of sample means approximates a normal curve (this is called the *central limit theorem*), and we know that 68% of the area of a normal curve is found between one standard deviation below the mean and one standard deviation above the mean.

It turns out that you do not need to collect those additional 99 samples, calculate each mean value, and then obtain the standard deviation of those means—that is, you don't need to get the standard error of the mean by brute force. You can estimate that standard error by means of this formula:

```
Standard Error = Standard Deviation / ( N ^ 0.5 )
```

In English, that says that the standard error of the mean equals the sample's standard deviation divided by the square root of the sample size, N.

You can tinker with the confidence interval's attributes, and most statisticians do so. For example, you could change the original 68% confidence interval to a 95% confidence interval by multiplying the size of the standard error by 1.96. Accumulating probabilities from 1.96 standard errors below the mean to 1.96 standard errors above the mean accounts for 95% of the area under a normal curve.

Frequentists also have a particular way of defining what a confidence interval returns. Suppose that you have calculated a 95% confidence interval around your sample mean of 120, and that the interval extends from 115 to 125. Is the probability therefore 95% that the population mean is captured in the 115 to 125 interval?

No. The probability is either 100% or 0% that a population mean is captured by a confidence interval constructed around a given sample mean. Either it's within the brackets or it isn't. What *is* true is that 95 of 100 of those 95% confidence intervals—imaginary as 99 of them may be—capture the true population mean. It simply makes sense to decide that your sample and its interval comprise one of the 95 intervals that capture the population mean, rather than one of the 5 that don't.

Confidence intervals aren't perfect. But as John Tukey wrote, they help to "make clear the essential 'smudginess' of experimental knowledge."

Applying `qbeta` to Confidence Intervals

R's `qbeta` function is almost perfectly suited to calculating basic confidence intervals. There's no need to calculate the standard error, nor to multiply the standard error to get the probability you want for the confidence interval, nor to appeal to the central limit theorem to justify the use of the normal curve as a reference distribution. There is some preparation that Bayes requires of you, but it's pretty quick and easy.

Suppose that you take a random sample of 1,000 registered voters in a particular voting district and asked each subject, among other things, who they will vote for in the next election to the House of Representatives. Four hundred seventy say they'll vote for the Republican and 530 for another party's candidate.

You want to put a 90% confidence interval around the sample mean of 47% Republican votes, to see whether the confidence interval's upper boundary falls below 50%. In that case, the Republican candidate would be unlikely to win a majority but might win a plurality. R can give you the points that bracket a 90% confidence interval given your sample data. Because you want a 90% interval, and a symmetric one at that, you want the interval to start at 5% and end at 95%. On the basis of the data from your survey, the sample value of 47% that say they'll vote Republican is expected to come in below the lower bracket of the 90% confidence interval 5% of the time, and above the upper bracket 5% of the time.

That accounts for 5% plus 5% of the total probability of 100%, leaving 90% accounted for within the confidence interval. The lower and upper brackets are calculated using `qbeta` as shown in Figure 3.12.

Figure 3.12
You can also use the `lower.tail` and `log.p` arguments to control the location and spread of the function's results.

```
R R Console
> qbeta(.05, 470, 530)
[1] 0.4440847
> qbeta(.95, 470, 530)
[1] 0.4959836
>
```

So with these data, the lower and upper bounds of the 90% confidence interval are 0.4441 and 0.4960. The 90% confidence interval fails to span the 0.5000 criterion, and therefore only the plurality remains plausible. Only if the lower bound of a confidence interval exceeded 0.5000 could you conclude with 90% confidence that the Republican has a majority in the population of voters.

The other side of the coin is that the 90% interval does not span 0.5000, so you can't expect an outright win based on these data—not on the basis of a 90% confidence interval.

Applying BETA.INV to Confidence Intervals

Excel also makes it straightforward to calculate confidence intervals based on Bayesian methods. In R, you submit a probability to `qbeta` and get a quantile back. In Excel, you submit a probability to BETA.INV and get a quantile back. Figure 3.13 shows the basic data in row 3, the lower boundary (result and function) in row 8, and the upper boundary (result and function) in row 10.

Figure 3.13
The lower and upper bounds of the confidence interval are in cells B8 and B10.

	A	B	C
1			
2	N	Republican	Other
3	1000	470	530
4			
5			
6			
7		90% confidence interval	
8		0.4440847	=BETA.INV(0.05,470,530)
9			
10		0.4959836	=BETA.INV(0.95,470,530)

Compare the results shown for R in Figure 3.12 with the results for Excel in Figure 3.13. They are identical, despite the major differences in the routes taken to reach the results.

Summary

In Bayesian analysis, you're responsible for defining the distributional nature of the various sources of information, whether prior or likelihood. This means that you are in a position to tell the software that the numbers are distributed normally or binomially, or discretely or continuously, and so on. You're also able to specify the point to which the numbers tend centrally and their degree of spread.

All this means is that you need to choose the functions you use in your analysis with due care. You'll want to be sure of the type of distribution—discrete or continuous, for example—in use as you decide whether to use a function that assumes a beta distribution or one that assumes a binomial distribution. This is critical information for defining the grid.

The intent of Chapter 3 is to establish the distinction between continuous variables and discrete variables, along with the consequences for how the variables might be distributed if they are continuous rather than discrete. There are also consequences for the pertinent distributional functions, such as dbinom and dbeta, pbinom and pbeta, and so on. These issues are critical in the process of deriving a useful posterior distribution, which will often inform you of the most accurate result.

Grid approximation is the first step in the simplest method of computing posterior distributions, and is the step taken up in Chapter 4.

Grid Approximation and the Beta Distribution

Prior chapters have discussed, if just briefly, the method sometimes termed *grid approximation* and the numeric structures usually termed *binomial* and *beta distributions*. As useful as these tools and methods are, it's hard to see how useful grid approximation can be in the absence of a binomial or beta distribution, or a binomial distribution in the absence of a grid approximation. I'll try to start joining these concepts in this chapter.

More on Grid Approximation

In many applications of the methods collectively known as Bayesian techniques, the formal workflow often begins with one or more assumptions about the data. These assumptions might be well-founded conjectures, such as "A random sample of 13 cards from a new deck, excluding jokers, will include exactly four honor cards: an ace, a king, a queen, and a jack."

Or they might be little more than shots in the dark. Without initial data to work with, you sometimes must assign the same probability (often 1 or 0) to each of your prior estimates. In keeping with the Bayesian tradition of coining several terms for the same concept, this results in a *noninformative* or *uniform* or *flat prior*, such as the one shown in Figure 4.1. Then your starting assumptions are virtually certain to be wrong, but at least you won't be deliberately backing the wrong horse.

Figure 4.1
Using grid approximation, this is how the initial prior might appear on an Excel worksheet.

	A	B	C	D	E	F	G	H	I
1	Alpha		1	Beta	1				
2									
3	Quantiles	=BETA.DIST (@Quantiles,Alpha,Beta,FALSE)							
4	0.05	1							
5	0.1	1							
6	0.15	1							
7	0.2	1							
8	0.25	1							
9	0.3	1							
10	0.35	1							
11	0.4	1							
12	0.45	1							
13	0.5	1							
14	0.55	1							
15	0.6	1							
16	0.65	1							
17	0.7	1							
18	0.75	1							
19	0.8	1							
20	0.85	1							
21	0.9	1							
22	0.95	1							

Figure 4.1 shows a grid. It is defined by the quantiles in column A and by the values in column B that the analyst has selected. It's called a grid because it looks like one: if you rotated column A and column B counterclockwise by 90 degrees, things would appear a little clearer. It would look similar to a frequency distribution, with the quantiles across the bottom and the frequency of the observations defining the height of each column. The point is that in this configuration, the *grid approximates* a frequency distribution.

In Figure 4.1, the value 1 is assigned to each quantile in the grid. As it happens, you can obtain that sequence of 1s as your grid's initial prior by setting both alpha and beta in the Beta distribution to 1. That is, in R, you might use the dbeta function in this way:

```
dbeta(quantiles, 1, 1)
```

in which the second and third arguments set the function's alpha and beta arguments, respectively, to 1. Or if you were using Excel, you could use this function:

```
=BETA.DIST(@quantiles, 1, 1, FALSE)
```

In either case, the function will return a sequence of 1s to your grid. (However, because it's your initial prior, you could just as well set each quantile's prior value to 1 using a less sophisticated procedure, such as selecting a worksheet cell and entering 1.)

Setting the Prior

Still, there will often be *some* basis, other than a random scattering of 1s, for the initial values of the first prior in a Bayesian analysis. The results of exit polling, mortality rates for different surgical procedures, the probability of arrest on a moving violation by driver ethnicity—if a research question is worth investigating at all, then it's likely that you can find some sort of preliminary information, wrong though it may be, regarding the frequency of occurrence of different outcomes.

I have set up the analyses in Figures 4.1 through 4.7 in the same way. Each figure shows an Excel chart of the beta distribution as the values for alpha and beta are incremented. In each figure:

- Cell B1 contains a value for alpha. The cell itself is named Alpha, and the name's scope is limited to that particular worksheet.

- Cell E1 contains a value for beta. The cell itself is named Beta, and again the name's scope is limited to that particular worksheet.

- The range A4:A24 contains the values of the quantiles. The range itself is named Quantiles, and the name's scope is again the worksheet that contains it. In some cases the number of rows in the range varies because the beta distribution cannot always deal with arguments of 0.0 or 1.0.

- Each row in column B contains the following formula, which makes use of the defined names scoped to the worksheet that contains the names (in other words, there are no workbook-level names):

```
=BETA.DIST(@Quantiles,Alpha,Beta,FALSE)
```

The implicit intersection operator, @, shows that the value in Quantiles, found in the same row as each BETA.DIST function, is used as that function's first argument. See the sidebar in Chapter 3 for more detailed information about the implicit intersection operator.

- The FALSE value, which is the fourth of four required arguments to the BETA.DIST function, merely tells the function whether to return the cumulative area (the total of all quantiles up to and including the present one) or the probability density function (PDF—the area associated with the current quantile only).

When you work with dbeta, dbinom, or BETA.DIST, keep in mind that the functions return the distribution of successes and failures (alpha and beta) across a range of probabilities defined by the quantiles. For example, when you're working with these functions, there is no need to multiply a likelihood estimate by the new prior to get a new posterior. Simply by submitting a probability from the prior grid, Alpha, Beta, and a cumulative argument if necessary, you get those posterior values directly from the beta or binomial function, whether from R or Excel.

Using the Results of the Beta Function

What do the results of the beta function tell you? They tell you the *relative* size of an effect (such as the probability of contracting a disease or of a successful ad campaign on a product's market share) on different outcomes. For example, an ad campaign might change the probability of a prospect being below the first quartile from 15% to 10%.

> **NOTE**
>
> It's easy to get confused by the prevalence of the percentages in this sort of analysis. The quantiles that structure your grid (the 8th percentile, the 3rd quartile, the median) are directly related to the proportion of area under the curve and between any two quantiles. The quantiles divide the horizontal axis of a curve into (typically) unequally spaced boundaries, so the miles a car has been driven in a week might be divided into segments such as these: 100 to 200, 200 to 250, 250 to 280, and so on. But the percentage of measures that populate each segment are invariant from sample to sample, even though the quantiles move to accommodate varying proportions of data.

As you'll see, as you iterate through the steps in a Bayesian procedure, errors in the initial prior are fairly quickly corrected. This is likely to occur when the number of cases in the likelihood is substantially greater than the number of cases in the prior—in that event, you have what's termed a *weak prior*, as distinct from a *strong prior*, which could easily have more cases than the likelihood.

To start, define a grid to hold the data as it comes in. You would typically do that by structuring an array, in a range of Excel worksheet cells or in a vector in R's workspace. In this example, these locations will hold the results of the initial prior *and* the cumulative results of subsequent sampling. (This grid doesn't necessarily do that sort of double duty, but it can be convenient for it to do so, particularly if you're writing code that will perform the analysis rather than keeping all the calculations on a worksheet.)

Figure 4.1 shows one way that a simple grid might appear in an Excel worksheet, including the quantiles that give structure to the grid, the initial prior values assigned to it, and the posterior values. (I'm omitting the likelihood modification here to emphasize other aspects of the grid. You'll see how likelihood fits in with priors and posteriors a little later in this chapter.)

Figures 4.1 through 4.7 show how the shape of the beta distribution can change along with increments to the `alpha` and `beta` parameters. In Figure 4.1, the range A4:A22 contains the quantiles that divide the beta distribution into, in this example, 20 segments: 0 to .05, .05 to .10, .10 to .15, and so on through .95 to 1.0. The choice of how many quantiles to call for is largely subjective.

Tracking the Shape and Location of the Distribution

Typically, each quantile is represented on a chart by its own point. You want enough quantiles to depict a chart of the beta distribution accurately. But, particularly with an analysis such as this one that calls for just one parameter, you can afford to specify plenty of quantiles: such an analysis completes within a few seconds at most. I called for 20 quantiles in this example.

Figure 4.1 is not a useful depiction of how a Bayesian analysis can help you understand an event, or a sequence of events. The values assigned to `alpha` and `beta` are simply too small, at 1.0 each, for the charted distribution to be at all informative. But you still need a starting point, if only to see how a change in `alpha` or `beta` can alter the appearance of the chart and the information it conveys. Compare the chart in Figure 4.1 with the one in Figure 4.2.

Figure 4.2

As soon as you move off a noninformative prior (such as `alpha` = `beta` = 1) the resulting chart begins to communicate useful information.

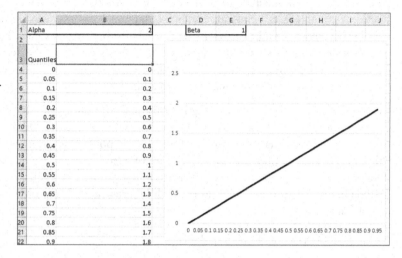

As you view the data and charts in Figures 4.1 through 4.7, keep these points in mind:

- From one figure to the next, the values of `alpha` or `beta` are incremented, and therefore the appearance of the chart changes from one figure to the next. Compare Figure 4.1 with Figure 4.2. Incrementing `alpha` results in the mode of the curve moving to the right, and incrementing `beta` moves the mode to the left. It helps to remember that `alpha` is usually construed as a measure of successes and `beta` as a measure of failures.

- The value of the curve's mode increases whenever either `alpha` or `beta` is incremented. Diminishing returns from increasing either `alpha` or `beta` have an effect: the greater the total of `alpha` and `beta`, the smaller the effect that adding to either parameter has on the shape and location of the curve.

- The more data that enters the function via either `alpha` or `beta`, the more closely the curve centers around the population value that you're trying to identify.

Inventorying the Necessary Functions

Let's start, as the previous chapter did, with a brief review of the pertinent worksheet functions in Excel and R. Just two functions in Excel have to do with the binomial distribution (apart from legacy functions): `BINOM.DIST`, which returns information about the area under the distribution's curve, and `BINOM.INV`, which returns information about the categories—or *quantiles*—that comprise the curve. Analogous functions in R include (but are not limited to) `dbinom` and `qbinom`.

The pattern that Excel uses for the beta distribution is similar to that of R's dbeta function. Excel offers a BETA.DIST function, which returns an area associated with a quantile, and a BETA.INV function, which returns information about the quantile associated with an area.

The underlying difference between the distributions is that the binomial functions, whether Excel's, R's, Python's, or some other source of binomial analysis, are intended for use with distributions that are built with variables that take on one of two values. Each value is discrete. Curious about a six-sided die, you roll it 10 times, counting the number of times it comes up 6 and the number of times it comes up some other value. You run the number of sixes and the number of "not-sixes" through a binomial function.

On the other hand, your interest might focus on a continuous variable such as body weight rather than on a discrete variable such as rolling boxcars. That calls for a beta function, not a binomial. Anything that weighs 105 pounds has more weight than something that weighs 104 pounds. But a coin flip of heads is just the other side of one of tails. The same is true of boxcars and snake eyes. Blood pressure is a continuous variable, and a systolic blood pressure of 129.5 has as much inherent meaning as either 129 or 130. Use a beta function.

Compare Figure 4.2 with Figure 4.3.

Figure 4.3
The total of alpha and beta, while still very small, is now large enough to convey some useful information.

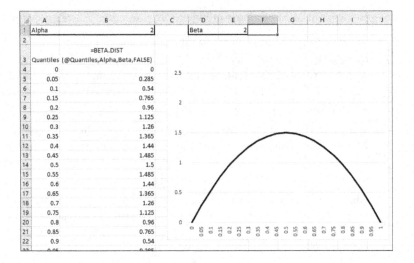

The pattern that Excel uses for the beta distribution is similar to that for the binomial. Excel offers a BETA.DIST function, which returns an area associated with a quantile, and a BETA.INV function, which returns information about the quantile associated with an area.

Figure 4.4, compared with Figure 4.3, shows how a chart can provide a better sense of the distribution as the number of cases increases.

Figure 4.4
With an `alpha` that's larger than `beta` and a total that's greater than 2, the curve starts to lean to the right.

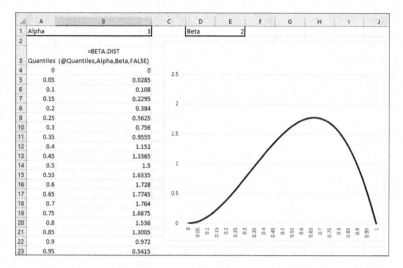

As the amount of available data increases, the curve starts to gain accuracy about the proportion of trials that you can expect to be successful or unsuccessful. Figures 4.4 and 4.5 show that, although you can't be certain of it yet, the distribution is likely to be negatively skewed (or skewed left).

Figure 4.5
`alpha` continues to increase and the curve bends further right. The total of `alpha` plus `beta` continues to increase and the curve grows taller.

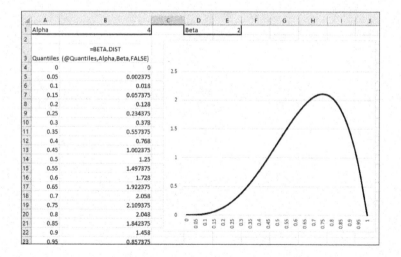

Adding more and more data to the model is like squeezing an open tube of toothpaste. The pressure pushes more of the available area toward the center and, to make room, the curve's height increases.

In contrast to prior figures, Figure 4.6 shows that incrementing `beta` nudges the curve to the left.

Figure 4.6
The value of beta increases by 1 from Figure 4.5, and the curve shifts left.

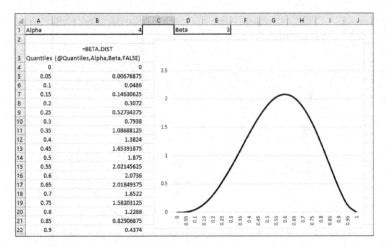

The curve's height increases, but only slightly because the leftward shift results in a fatter left tail.

Figure 4.7 shows how the curve's central tendency has started to assert itself.

Figure 4.7
Notice how much more closely the data clusters around its mode compared to a model with fewer observations, such as Figure 4.4.

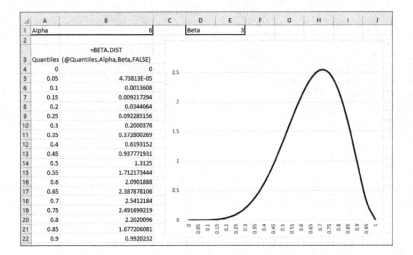

All we've really done in moving from the chart in Figure 4.1 to Figure 4.7 is to increase either alpha or beta by 1 in each figure. Still, hidden inside that process and inside the BETA.DIST functions are the classic steps in a Bayesian analysis:

1. Get a prior, either an initial prior or the previous step's posterior. This is what happens when you decide to add new data to an existing model; specifically, in this example when you add 1 to the current value of either alpha or beta.

2. Combine the new with the existing data. When you add 1 to either `alpha` or `beta`, you are updating the likelihood.

3. Calculate the new model (or, if you prefer, the new posterior distribution) based on the prior and the likelihood. The preceding example doesn't show this happen directly, but you can see the results in the new values that `BETA.DIST` or `dbeta` return to the grid.

Looking Behind the Curtains

I want to provide a couple of demonstrations of processes used in grid approximations that don't usually get the attention they deserve. The first concerns rescaling the posterior distribution so that its elements sum to 1.00 (or if you prefer, 100%).

The second concerns the combination of distributions, in particular the combination of the prior with the likelihood to bring about a posterior distribution, and the rescaling of a raw posterior distribution so that the probability of the quantiles sums to 1.0.

Standardizing the Grid

Let's start with a demonstration in R. I'll use a small data set, and if you wish to replicate it using a larger one, it's pretty easy to do so.

Neither the `library` function nor the `tibble` function at the end of the code is strictly necessary, but I—along with a lot of other users—find them useful. If you wish to use them in following this demonstration, you should first install the tibble package using the Install package(s) item in R's Packages menu.

```
library(tibble)

# Establish quantiles for a grid
grid_qs <- seq(0, 1, by = 0.25)
grid_qs
# Get the prior density for each value on the grid
prior <- dbeta(grid_qs, 31, 27)
prior
# Get the likelihood for each value on the grid
likelihood <- dbinom(8, 20, prob = grid_qs)
likelihood
# Multiply to get the posterior
raw_posterior <- prior * likelihood
raw_posterior
# Note that raw_posterior sums to 0.632, not 1.00
sum(raw_posterior)
# Rescale posterior so that its sum is 1.00
rescaled_posterior <- raw_posterior / sum(raw_posterior)
rescaled_posterior
sum(rescaled_posterior)
# Prepare a data frame with pertinent values
grid_app_df <- data.frame(grid_qs, prior, likelihood,
  raw_posterior, rescaled_posterior)
grid_app_df
```

```
# Prepare a table with pertinent values
grid_data <- tibble(grid = grid_qs,
 prior = prior,
 likelihood = likelihood,
 `prior x likelihood` = raw_posterior,
 posterior = rescaled_posterior)
grid_data
```

The code is in a text file named *R code for grid approximation.txt*. You can run the code in R by copying it, switching to R, choosing File, New Script, and pasting the code into R's Untitled – R Editor window. If you are typing the code rather than using a copy-and-paste procedure, be sure to omit the line continuation characters toward the end of the code. Then, choose Run All from R's Edit menu. Here's what shows up in the console. (Because it shows up in the console, each executable or comment statement begins with a > symbol. Results returned by functions do not begin with the > symbol.)

```
> library(tibble)

> # Establish quantiles for a grid
> grid_qs <- seq(0, 1, by = 0.25)
> grid_qs
[1] 0.00 0.25 0.50 0.75 1.00
> # Get the prior density for each value on the grid
> prior <- dbeta(grid_qs, 31, 27 )
> prior
[1] 0.0000000000 0.0001854631 5.2575660200 0.0150225141 0.0000000000
> # Get the likelihood for each value on the grid
> likelihood <- dbinom(8, 20, prob = grid_qs)
> likelihood
[1] 0.0000000000 0.0608866892 0.1201343536 0.0007516875 0.0000000000
> # Multiply to get the posterior
> raw_posterior <- prior * likelihood
> raw_posterior
[1] 0.000000e+00 1.129224e-05 6.316143e-01 1.129224e-05 0.000000e+00
> # Note that raw_posterior sums to 0.576, not 1.00
> sum(raw_posterior)
[1] 0.6316369
> # Rescale posterior so that its sum is 1.00
> rescaled_posterior <- raw_posterior / sum(raw_posterior)
> rescaled_posterior
[1] 0.000000e+00 1.787773e-05 9.999642e-01 1.787773e-05 0.000000e+00
> sum(rescaled_posterior)
[1] 1
> # Prepare a data frame with pertinent values
> grid_app_df <- data.frame(grid_qs, prior, likelihood,
+   raw_posterior, rescaled_posterior)
> grid_app_df
  grid_qs        prior  likelihood raw_posterior rescaled_posterior
1    0.00 0.0000000000 0.0000000000  0.000000e+00       0.000000e+00
2    0.25 0.0001854631 0.0608866892  1.129224e-05       1.787773e-05
3    0.50 5.2575660200 0.1201343536  6.316143e-01       9.999642e-01
4    0.75 0.0150225141 0.0007516875  1.129224e-05       1.787773e-05
5    1.00 0.0000000000 0.0000000000  0.000000e+00       0.000000e+00
> # Prepare a table with pertinent values
> grid_data <- tibble(grid = grid_qs,
```

```
+ prior = prior,
+ likelihood = likelihood,
+ `prior x likelihood` = raw_posterior,
+ posterior = rescaled_posterior)
> grid_data
# A tibble: 5 x 5
   grid    prior likelihood `prior x likelihood` posterior
   <dbl>   <dbl>   <dbl>                  <dbl>     <dbl>
1  0       0       0                       0          0
2  0.25  0.000185  0.0609               0.0000113  0.0000179
3  0.5   5.26      0.120                0.632      1.00
4  0.75  0.0150    0.000752             0.0000113  0.0000179
5  1       0       0                       0          0
>
```

> **TIP**
> If you don't find a Run All command in R's Edit menu, make sure that the Untitled – R Editor window is active by clicking in it.

R executes the code it finds in the Untitled – R Editor window and displays the results in the Console.

There are several points to note about the code just given. One is that it calculates two versions of the posterior. The version that the code terms *raw_posterior* in the data frame named *grid_app_df* (and that it names `prior x likelihood` in the tibble) totals to 0.632. The tibble contains six columns, and the fifth displays the five *raw_posterior* values that, down the grid, again total to 0.632.

That total is inconvenient. The values that comprise the posterior are supposed to be proportions, or percentages, that total to 1.0 or 100%. That's why the code totals the raw values returned by the product of the prior and the likelihood, and then divides that total into each raw posterior value. The result is a vector that the code names *rescaled_posterior*, or simply *posterior*.

The rescaled values in that vector do sum to 1.0, and the individual values bear the same relationship to one another as do the values in the raw_posterior. For example, the ratio of the third element in the raw_posterior to its second element is 55929.20 to 1, and the same ratio for the rescaled_posterior is 55865.92 to 1. (The vanishingly small difference is due to the errors of rounding that one inevitably encounters with integral calculus.)

You will probably find that plenty of sources of material on Bayesian methods refer to the process of rescaling a raw_posterior in this fashion as "standardizing" or as "normalizing." In most cases, you can avoid having to go through the extra steps of standardizing by setting the quantiles to percentiles. That is, use code similar to the following when you're structuring the grid:

```
grid_qs <- seq(0, 1, by = 0.01)
```

In most cases, this will cause the elements of the grid to total to 1.00 or 100%, and you won't have to go through the extra steps of converting a raw posterior to a standardized posterior. You generally want a standardized posterior, and one good way to ensure that is to arrange 100 quantiles. Any other number of quantiles results in a grid that sums to a total other than 1.00, but you can always fix that by standardizing the posterior.

Combining Distributions

Nearly any book on Bayesian analysis stresses that one of its steps, when you're working with proportions instead of integer counts, is to multiply a prior by a likelihood. This is just one way in which distributions can be combined, but it's a critical approach in Bayesian analysis.

You need two distributions of data, with each distribution organized by the variable that defines the quantiles. For example, the prior distribution might have eight records in the segment that runs from 0% to 10%. It might have another four records in the segment that runs from 10% to 20%, and so on.

You should have the likelihood data arranged in the same fashion, with the same quantiles that you used on the prior distribution and sorted in the same way that the prior distribution is sorted.

One way to proceed at this point it is to multiply the percent in each quantile of the prior by the percent in the associated quantile of the likelihood distribution. The resulting product of the two distributions has the same quantiles as the prior and the likelihood. The contents of each quantile are the product of the value in the prior for that quantile and the value in the likelihood for the same quantile.

Figure 4.8 demonstrates this.

Figure 4.8
The prior, likelihood, and (raw) posterior distributions taken from R, and the multiplication as done in Excel.

	A	B	C	D	E	F
1	> prior			R results		
2						
3	[1]	0.00000000	0.00011280	4.79637602	0.02740950	0.00000000
4						
5	> likelihood					
6	[1]	0.00000000	0.06088669	0.12013435	0.00075169	0.00000000
7						
8	> raw_posterior					
9	[1]	0.00000000	0.00000687	0.57620950	0.00002060	0.00000000
10						
11			Raw posterior (by multiplication in Excel)			
12	[1]	0.00000000	0.00000687	0.57620953	0.00002060	0.00000000
13						

B12 fx =B3*B6

Each distribution is divided into five areas, established by the four equidistant quantiles of 0.25, 0.50, 0.75, and 1.00. The contents of each area are found in columns B through F. To get the raw posterior distribution, multiply the prior's area by the corresponding area in the likelihood distribution. Your results may vary slightly. In R, of course, you can get not just the single result but the full one much more simply and quickly by telling R to multiply the prior distribution by the likelihood:

```
> raw_posterior <- prior * likelihood
```

However, both Excel and R, provide an alternative method for getting the product of two distributions. Even if you never employ this method, you should understand what it does so you can properly follow some code that *does* use it. It's mainly a matter of carefully managing the arguments to the functions BETA.DIST and BINOM.DIST, or dbeta and dbinom.

Suppose that you want to multiply a prior by a likelihood using R. You might find it convenient to use R's dbeta function to do so. Recall from earlier chapters that the dbeta function takes, among other arguments, one that the R documentation refers to as shape1 and another called shape2. The same documentation states that both shape1 and shape2 are non-negative parameters of the beta distribution. (Microsoft Excel's documentation refers to these two arguments as alpha and beta, and defines them only as required parameters of the distribution. No help there either.)

You can think of them, quite literally, as two sides of the same coin. You could treat the number of coin flips that come up heads as alpha (or as shape1), and the number of flips that come up tails as beta (or as shape2). Wins and losses. Gets sick, stays well. Systolic higher than 125.2, lower than or equal to 125.2.

There's an alternative to multiplying the prior times the likelihood, which is available in both R and in Excel. Suppose first that you are using R, not Excel. Your prior is defined by an object that you have named prior_approx, and the likelihoods associated with each quantile in the grid are collectively named like_approx. Both prior_approx and like_approx have been established using dbeta. (That's certainly no requirement, however. It wouldn't be at all unusual to use dbeta to establish the prior and dbinom to establish the likelihood due to their conjugate families.)

Your goal is to combine prior_approx with like_approx without actually multiplying them together. To do so, you need to add the value of shape1 in prior_approx to the value of shape1 in like_approx. You also need to add the value of shape2 in prior_approx to the value of shape2 in like_approx. Then call dbeta again, this time with the sums of the two parameters.

For example, suppose that you defined prior_approx in this way:

```
prior_approx <- dbeta(x = quantiles, shape1 = 7, shape2 = 9)
```

and like_approx as follows:

```
like_approx <- dbeta(x = quantiles, shape1 = 10, shape2 = 12)
```

Then the posterior is given by:

```
raw_posterior <- dbeta(x = quantiles, shape1 = 7 + 10, shape2 = 9 + 12)
```

or simply:

```
raw_posterior <- dbeta(x = quantiles, shape1 = 17, shape2 = 21)
```

The following shows much of the code given in the previous section, but it adds, simply for comparison, the code that incorporates the dbeta function to calculate the posterior—both the raw version termed alt_posterior and the standardized version termed dbeta_posterior.

```
> # Establish quantiles for a grid

> grid_qs <- seq(0, 1, by = 0.25)
> grid_qs
[1] 0.00 0.25 0.50 0.75 1.00
>
> # Get the prior density for each value on the grid
> prior <- dbeta(grid_qs, shape1 = 31, shape2 = 27)
> prior
[1] 0.0000000000 0.0001854631 5.2575660200 0.0150225141 0.0000000000
>
> # Get the likelihood for each value on the grid
> likelihood <- dbinom(x = 8, size = 20, prob = grid_qs)
> likelihood
[1] 0.0000000000 0.0608866892 0.1201343536 0.0007516875 0.0000000000
>
> # Multiply to get the posterior
> raw_posterior <- prior * likelihood
> raw_posterior
[1] 0.000000e+00 1.129224e-05 6.316143e-01 1.129224e-05 0.000000e+00
>
> # Standardize the posterior
> rescaled_posterior <- raw_posterior/sum(raw_posterior)
> rescaled_posterior
[1] 0.000000e+00 1.787773e-05 9.999642e-01 1.787773e-05 0.000000e+00
>
> # Calculate the posterior using dbeta
> alt_posterior <- dbeta(grid_qs, shape1 = 31 + 8, shape2 = 27 + 12)
> alt_posterior
[1] 0.0000000000 0.0001255809 7.0241767538 0.0001255809 0.0000000000
>
> # Standardize dbeta's version of posterior
> dbeta_posterior <- alt_posterior/sum(alt_posterior)
> dbeta_posterior
[1] 0.000000e+00 1.787773e-05 9.999642e-01 1.787773e-05 0.000000e+00
```

The important comparison to make here is between the variable named rescaled_posterior and the one named dbeta_posterior. Each of the elements in the former variable is precisely equal to the corresponding element in the latter variable. For example, comparing the second element in both variables, 1.787773e-05 equals 1.787773e-05.

The point is that you can obtain the raw posterior in two ways:

■ By multiplying the prior by the likelihood: above, to get raw_posterior, given that you are using percentages.

■ By using dbeta on the total number of "wins" (shape1) and "losses" (shape2): above, to get alt_posterior, given that you are using raw counts

The raw density values that result will be different for the two procedures, but the density values should be identical in either version of the standardized posterior.

Combining Distributions in Excel

Figure 4.9 shows the results of a similar analysis in more compact form, along with the formulas and functions for Excel. Compare the results in Figure 4.8, derived from R, with those in Figure 4.9, derived from Excel.

Figure 4.9
The prior, likelihood, and both the raw and the standardized distributions taken from Excel.

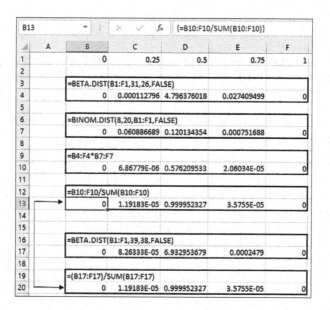

In Figure 4.9, row 3 shows the formulas, entered in row 4, that represent the conjugate prior for the analysis. Conforming to the syntax for the BETA.DIST function, the formula specifies B1:F1 as the range that contains the quantiles; 31 and 26 as the values for alpha and beta, and the keyword FALSE to indicate that we do *not* want a cumulative result. That formula is array-entered in row 4, which then returns the values for the prior distribution.

Row 7 displays the formula that returns the binomial distribution for the likelihood that's associated with the prior in row 4. We have already discussed that the syntax is somewhat different for the BETA.DIST and the BINOM.DIST functions in Excel.

In this BINOM.DIST function, we start out with alpha, the number of successes, and 20, the total number of trials. As before, the quantiles are in the range B1:F1. Once again we do not want a cumulative distribution, so we use FALSE as the fourth argument to BINOM.DIST.

In row 10, we have the result of multiplying the individual values in B4:F4 by the individual values in B7:F7. For example, C4 times C7 equals the value shown in C10. As the product of the prior and the likelihood, row 10 contains the raw posterior for this step in the analysis.

Row 13 contains the formula that divides the values in B10 through F10—that is, the raw posterior—by the sum of those values. The result is the standardized version of the raw posterior, one that can be compared with another method of deriving the standardized posterior. (More importantly, the standardized posterior maintains the relative size of the values in the raw version of the posterior.)

Avoiding a Trap

Now, there is a danger hidden in the use of dbeta—and of BETA.DIST, for that matter—to combine distributions as shown above. Here is how the R code calculates the prior:

```
prior <- dbeta(grid_qs, shape1 = 31, shape2 = 27)
```

Notice that the code uses this dbinom function to calculate the likelihood:

```
likelihood <- dbinom(x = 8, size = 20, prob = grid_qs)
```

The final two arguments to the dbeta function are the number of successes (31) and the number of failures (27). But the corresponding two arguments to the dbinom function are the number of successes (8) and the total number of trials (20), *not* the number of failures. The dbeta function expects you to provide the total number of successes (here, 31 + 8, or 39) and the total number of failures (here, 27 plus 20 minus 8, or 39—that is, 27 prior failures plus the total number of likelihood trials minus the number of likelihood successes).

> NOTE
>
> Another way to bear this issue in mind is as follows.
>
> When a developer designs a function in R, the developer usually supplies a list of arguments that the function can accept and use to complete the function's purpose. When a user employs that function, the user must normally supply values that the code will treat as the function's arguments. The user can supply those values in one of three general ways. Let's consider the dbinom function, for example, where R's documentation gives the density of a discrete event as
>
> ```
> dbinom(x, size, prob, log = FALSE)
> ```
>
> where x is the number of successes, size is the number of trials, prob is the probability of success on any given trial, and log specifies whether probabilities are specified in logarithmic form. The first of the three general methods of supplying the values of the arguments is the exact form:
>
> 1. Full, exact name. The user can specify an argument's value by supplying the argument's full name and value anywhere in the argument list. Here is a typical example:
>
>    ```
>    dbinom(x = 5, size = 10, prob = .5, log = FALSE)
>    ```
>
>   Notice that the arguments are given with the same exact names as specified in the documentation. In this case, the arguments can be supplied in any order, such as x, log, prob, and size.

> **2.** Partial match. The user supplies argument names that are abbreviations of the argument's formal, exact name. For example, the example given for the full name method could use the partial match method as follows:
>
> ```
> dbinom(x = 5, s = 10, prob = .5, log = FALSE)
> ```
>
> The letter *s* is a partial match with *size*.
>
> **3.** Argument order. The user can dispense entirely with the argument names and simply supply their values, as long as the order of the values in the call to the function matches the order of the arguments in the function's definition.
>
> (I have deferred discussion of this issue until now to avoid mixing distributional concepts such as discrete versus continuous distributions with typing techniques such as abbreviations of function names.)
>
> Continuing the present example:
>
> ```
> dbinom(5, 10, .5,  FALSE)
> ```
>
> All three usages, employed properly, return the same result, and usages may be mixed in the same function call. The full, exact name approach is the safest, and the most tedious of the three. The argument-only approach can be a lot quicker from the keyboard, but it is also most susceptible to problems with the argument list. That's especially the case when the formal names given by the documentation provide little clue as to the meaning of each argument. A good example is the documentation for dbeta, where two of the arguments are named shape1 and shape2.

Still in Figure 4.9, row 16 shows the formula that is entered in row 17, making use of the BETA.DIST function to avoid having to multiply the prior times the likelihood explicitly. Instead of the multiplication, shown in row 10, we will use BETA.DIST directly but accumulate the records from the likelihood into the arguments for the beta function. So, alpha in row 17 is 39, which is the sum of alpha for the prior, 31, plus alpha for the likelihood, 8. And the value of beta in row 17 is 38, because as you'll see shortly, we do not arrive at the value of beta of 38 in the same fashion that we arrived at the alpha of 39.

The BINOM.DIST function, used in row 7, calls for the number 8 as alpha, the number of successes, and the number 20, not as the number of failures but as the total number of trials. But the BETA.DIST function, which we're about to use to calculate the posterior, expects not the total number of trials but the number of failures to go along with the number of successes. In consequence, the third argument to BETA.DIST, row 17, is 26 + 12 or 38, not 57 + 20 or 77.

Notice that row 13 returns precisely the same values as row 20, demonstrating that the standardized version of the posterior created by multiplying the prior times the likelihood is equal to the standardized posterior created by the use of the BETA.DIST function.

I can tell you from bitter personal experience how easy it is to forget to change the number of trials used in the dbinom function to the number of failures implied by the combination of the number of successes with the total number of trials.

Moving from the Underlying Formulas to the Functions

Here's how the numbers work. Figure 4.10 shows how the complete grid moves from the underlying formula to the current prior.

Figure 4.10
How the prior and the likelihood values of alpha and beta are "added" to reach the posterior.

F14 =C14*D14/E14

	A	B	C	D	E	F	G	H
1–2	$\pi^{(a-1)}(1-\pi)^{(b-1)}/\beta(a,b)$							
3						Conjugate prior		
4	a =	5						
5	b =	8				By formula		By function
6								=BETA.DIST
7	π		$\pi^{(a-1)}$	$(1-\pi)^{(b-1)}$	β(a,b)	$\pi^{(a-1)}*(1-\pi)^{(b-1)}/\beta(a,b)$		(@p,a,b,FALSE)
8	0		0.0000	1.0000	0.0003	0.0000		0.0000
9	0.1		0.0001	0.4783	0.0003	0.1894		0.1894
10	0.2		0.0016	0.2097	0.0003	1.3288		1.3288
11	0.3		0.0081	0.0824	0.0003	2.6416		2.6416
12	0.4		0.0256	0.0280	0.0003	2.8379		2.8379
13	0.5		0.0625	0.0078	0.0003	1.9336		1.9336
14	0.6		0.1296	0.0016	0.0003	0.8409		0.8409
15	0.7		0.2401	0.0002	0.0003	0.2079		0.2079
16	0.8		0.4096	0.0000	0.0003	0.0208		0.0208
17	0.9		0.6561	0.0000	0.0003	0.0003		0.0003
18	1		1.0000	0.0000	0.0003	0.0000		0.0000

4

First, the formula for the conjugate prior is assembled in columns A through E of Figure 4.10. (This chapter discusses the notion of conjugate priors a little later on.)

$$\pi^{a}\,(1-\pi)^{b}/\beta\,(a,b)$$

where:

- π is a quantile such as 0.01, 0.10, or 0.25 that segments the total probability area.
- *a* is the number of successes.
- *b* is the number of failures.
- β is the beta function, defined as follows:

$$\beta(a,\,b) = \Gamma\,(a)\ *\ \Gamma\,(b)\ /\ \Gamma\,(a + b)$$

- Γ is the gamma function. Both Excel and R provide the gamma function.

The next step is to multiply the prior and the likelihood. Figure 4.11 shows how the prior and the likelihood are combined to result in the standardized posterior, which may be destined to act as the next prior.

Figure 4.11
Reaching an updated
posterior with grid
approximation.

D9		×	✓	fx	=B9*C9		

	A	B	C	D	E	F	G
1							
2	π	Conjugate Prior	Likelihood	Conjugate Prior * Likelihood	Standardized posterior	Posterior from BETA.DIST()	Standardized posterior
3	0	0.0000	0.0000	0.0000	0.0000	0.0000	0.0000
4	0.1	0.1894	0.0000	0.0000	0.0000	0.0000	0.0000
5	0.2	1.3288	0.0000	0.0000	0.0017	0.0171	0.0017
6	0.3	2.6416	0.0001	0.0002	0.0388	0.3883	0.0388
7	0.4	2.8379	0.0004	0.0010	0.1968	1.9680	0.1968
8	0.5	1.9336	0.0010	0.0019	0.3700	3.7001	0.3700
9	0.6	0.8409	0.0018	0.0015	0.2952	2.9520	0.2952
10	0.7	0.2079	0.0022	0.0005	0.0906	0.9060	0.0906
11	0.8	0.0208	0.0017	0.0000	0.0068	0.0683	0.0068
12	0.9	0.0003	0.0005	0.0000	0.0000	0.0002	0.0000
13	1	0.0000	0.0000	0.0000	0.0000	0.0000	0.0000
14							
15							
16	a =	5					
17	b =	8					
18	f =	7					
19	g =	3					

The formula for the likelihood is the familiar binomial distribution:

$$\pi^f (1-\pi)^g$$

where:

- π is as described just above, a quantile or vector of quantiles.
- f is the number of successes in the likelihood sample. If this were a prior rather than a likelihood, the symbol f would be replaced by the symbol a.
- g is the number of failures in the likelihood sample. If this were a prior rather than a likelihood, the symbol g would be replaced by the symbol b.

So, in Figure 4.11:

- A3:A13 contains the quantiles.
- B3:B13 contains the prior, calculated in Figure 4.10.
- C3:C13 contains the likelihood, based on $\pi, f,$ and g as just described.
- D3:D13 contains the raw product of the prior and the likelihood.
- E3:E13 contains the standardized product, obtained by dividing each raw product in D3:D13 by the sum of the raw product values.
- F3:F13 contains the raw posterior, calculated by passing alpha, beta, and π to BETA.DIST or, as we've seen, to the dbeta function in R.
- G3:G13 contains the standardized posterior, calculated by dividing each raw posterior value by their sum.

4

Let's take a closer look at the effect of multiplying the prior times the likelihood. Here's how it lays out, as a formula, rather than as either an R or an Excel function:

$$\pi^{a-1} (1-\pi)^{b-1} \pi^f (1-\pi)^g / \beta (a, b)$$

Or, simplifying:

$$\pi^{(a-1+f)} (1-\pi)^{(b-1+g)} / \beta (a, b)$$

What has happened in the simplification is as follows:

$$\pi^{(a-1+f)} \text{ replaces } \pi^{a-1} \text{ and } \pi^f$$

$$(1-\pi)^{(b-1+g)} \text{ replaces } (1-\pi)^{b-1} \text{ and } (1-\pi)^g$$

The two shape parameters for the likelihood, f and g, have indeed been added to the prior (as you're likely to read in other sources). However, f and g have been added to the *exponents* in the equations. Therefore, the effect of including the likelihood data via multiplication is to extend the number of times that the probability π (or 1 minus the probability) is multiplied by itself. All we are doing is increasing the size of the exponents.

This makes perfect sense when you consider that the probability of two independent events is simply their product. If X is the probability of an event occurring, then X^2 is the probability of X occurring, independently, twice. And in that case, the probability of X occurring independently a third time increases from X^2 to X^3.

Comparing Built-in Functions with Underlying Formulas

If you'd like to verify the relationship between calculating the prior from scratch using the underlying formula and calculating it using BETA.DIST or the dbeta function, that's easily done. With reference to Figure 4.11, pick a quantile such as the 0.6 for π in cell A9. The prior for this quantile is given by the following formula:

$$(0.6^{(a-1)})((1- 0.6)^{(b-1)}) / \beta (a, b)$$

where the values of a and b used in Figure 4.11 are 5 and 8, respectively. The denominator in the formula is the beta function, defined earlier as:

$$\beta (a, b) = \Gamma (a) * \Gamma (b) / \Gamma (a + b)$$

or, in pseudo-syntax:

```
β (a, b) = GAMMA(a) * GAMMA (b) / GAMMA (a + b)
```

to return 0.8409, the prior for p = 0.6 with a and b equal to 5 and 8. Compare the result with that returned in cell B9 by this function:

```
BETA.DIST(A9,a,b,FALSE)
```

You can proceed by checking the raw posterior shown in, say, cell D9 as 0.0015. The underlying formula is simply the prior times the likelihood: in the case of the 0.6 quantile, this is the result of B9*C9.

In a blank cell on Figure 4.11 or 4.12, where the names a, b, f, and g are scoped, enter this formula:

```
=(0.6^(a+f-1))*((1-A9)^(b+g-1))/(GAMMA(5)*GAMMA(8)/GAMMA(5+8))
```

which returns 0.0015, the same value as the product of the prior and the likelihood, B9*C9.

The equivalencies between the underlying formulas and the functions such as BETA.DIST or dbeta are summarized in Figure 4.12.

Figure 4.12
Test the equality with formulas such as =E16=D9.

| E16 | | f_x | =(A9^(a+f-1))*((1-A9)^(b+g-1))/(GAMMA(5)*GAMMA(8)/GAMMA(5+8)) | | | | | |

	A	B	C	D	E	F	G	H	I
1									
2	π	Conjugate Prior	Likelihood	Conjugate Prior * Likelihood	Standardized posterior	Posterior from BETA.DIST()	Standardized posterior		
3	0	0.0000	0.0000	0.0000	0.0000	0.0000	0.0000		
4	0.1	0.1894	0.0000	0.0000	0.0000	0.0000	0.0000		
5	0.2	1.3288	0.0000	0.0000	0.0017	0.0171	0.0017		
6	0.3	2.6416	0.0001	0.0002	0.0388	0.3883	0.0388		
7	0.4	2.8379	0.0004	0.0010	0.1968	1.9680	0.1968		
8	0.5	1.9336	0.0010	0.0019	0.3700	3.7001	0.3700		
9	0.6	0.8409	0.0018	0.0015	0.2952	2.9520	0.2952		
10	0.7	0.2073	0.0022	0.0005	0.0906	0.9060	0.0906		
11	0.8	0.0208	0.0017	0.0000	0.0068	0.0683	0.0068		
12	0.9	0.0003	0.0005	0.0000	0.0000	0.0002	0.0000		
13	1	0.0000	0.0000	0.0000	0.0000	0.0000	0.0000		
14									
15									
16	a =	5			0.8409	0.0015			
17	b =	8							
18	f =	7							
19	g =	3							

Understanding Conjugate Priors

When you multiply a distribution such as a prior by another distribution such as a likelihood, the result in Bayesian analysis might not be of the same type or family as the prior.

A family of distributions comprises distributions that share similar characteristics; for example, distributions of discrete variables such as the outcome of flipping a coin where there can be only two results, heads and tails. Other families of distributions include those that provide for an infinity of permissible outcomes and those that do not, and those that provide for both discrete and continuous measures.

In Bayesian analysis, you often find yourself multiplying a prior distribution by a likelihood. It turns out that is desirable for the result of the multiplication, the posterior, to belong to the same family as does the prior distribution. When this is the case, the prior and the posterior are termed *conjugates*, and the prior is frequently termed a *conjugate prior*.

That is a desirable state of affairs. When you have gathered more data as you iterate through the phases of the analysis, you might well want to use the posterior distribution as the prior to the next phase.

However, it is relatively difficult to find interesting problems that result in priors that follow a beta distribution. Historically, that situation limited the use of Bayesian analysis until an alternative to grid approximation could be found: one that did not necessitate the use of the beta distribution to describe the way that data span the distribution's range. In recent years, other methods such as Markov Chain Monte Carlo (MCMC) have been employed in place of reliance on conjugate priors, and the result has been considerably more use of Bayesian analysis than had earlier been the case.

Summary

When you multiply a distribution such as a prior by a likelihood, the result, in Bayesian analysis, might not be of the same type or family as the prior.

Matters become much simpler when the prior and the posterior are of the same distributional family. In that case, you do not need to jump through mathematical hoops to use the posterior distribution as the next prior. Those hoops, often termed open-form expressions, entail operations such as integration and differentiation, which can be expensive not only of computer time but of real time as well.

When a prior and its posterior do not belong to the same distributional family, when they are not conjugates, it might be necessary to resort to an open form of the distribution's equation. Closed-form expressions tend to be limited to equations that use straightforward arithmetic and trigonometry rather than more complex operations such as those employed in calculus.

One of the pairs of distributions that result in conjugate distributions is the beta combined with the binomial. When you multiply a beta by a binomial distribution the result is a conjugate prior: the posterior distribution is itself a beta distribution. That makes the coding and the math considerably less difficult.

This is not to say that the method of grid approximation does not have a place in Bayesian analysis. It does. It is well suited to straightforward problems that do not entail multiple variables, because grid approximation does not scale well. It becomes a relatively cumbersome tool when it's used in that sort of situation: when it is asked to provide an analysis of a design that calls for many variables. So, keep it in your toolkit, but be aware there can be stronger alternatives.

We'll start examining these alternatives to grid approximation in the next chapters.

Grid Approximation with Multiple Parameters

5

This is not meant to be a treatise on the use of VBA code—or R code for that matter—but if you are to understand what the code is doing it's necessary to get at least an overview of it. I'm presenting this coding example using a combination of an Excel worksheet and Visual Basic for Applications (VBA). Here's why:

It's generally acknowledged that VBA is not optimized for statistical analysis. Certainly, it's possible to carry out certain statistical procedures using VBA, but it's also true that many of those procedures require 10, 20, even 50 lines of code to accomplish something that a language such as R can accomplish in one or two statements.

Furthermore, the default installation of R on your computer provides you with a library of *compiled* functions. Compile-time errors have already been found and fixed. And VBA must often interpret statements that are executed repeatedly and that must be evaluated in each repeated instance. All this often requires much longer development time, and results in slower execution speed in VBA than is required in a language such as R's.

> **NOTE**
> I don't want to unduly alarm you. The code and data in this chapter run to completion in about 15 seconds on an HP laptop with an i5 core.

I could have made the VBA code that I discuss in this chapter much briefer. For example, there are two procedures that establish arrays of factor levels. I could have made do with just one procedure and arranged for the two arrays by means of arguments passed through that procedure.

However, that would have tended to focus your attention on trivialities such as arguments passed by reference versus those passed by value. The reason to spend time on this VBA code is that it tends to illuminate the rationale behind the analysis. Better that than to spend time and effort learning the niceties of a moribund coding language.

And there are several places in the code where I could have displayed user forms to pick up user input. Instead, that input was hard-coded, and you must modify the code in order to accommodate changes such as the location of information that you want to use. Again, though, I think it's more important to focus on the logic and the flow of the analysis than on the preparation of user-cordial code.

On the other hand, there must be 10 people who are familiar with VBA for every one person who is familiar with R's coding language. It's a lot easier to comprehend the purpose of a nested loop in VBA than it is to comprehend the purpose and result of R's SSA function—elegant as that function might be.

So, the reason that I include the following discussion of code, used by Bayesian analysis but written in VBA, is not to recommend that you adopt VBA in place of R or Python for statistical programming. The reason is that it's a lot easier to see what's going on in the code when you're familiar with that code's conventions and functions than otherwise. It's also handy that you can check the meaning of code that you have written for a complicated calculation by entering it as a formula in its own worksheet cell—that's a good way to check the correspondence between a known formula and a yet-to-be-tested snippet of code. That sort of development check is much easier to carry out in Excel than it is in R.

With that as rationale, let's take a look at a two-parameter Bayesian analysis using grid approximation written in VBA. Earlier chapters have focused on single-parameter analyses. One-parameter grid approximation is often much more straightforward to carry out, and just as accurate, as other methods, such as quadratic approximations and MCMC. My hope is that this will convince you to use quadratic approximations or, better, MCMC when your analysis is complicated enough to call for it.

Setting the Stage

Many variables of interest to scientists and statisticians are distributed as a normal or "bell" curve. (You are also likely to see such curves referred to in the literature as *Gaussian*.) These curves tend to be symmetric rather than skewed. It is also possible to specify their distributions with two numbers: a measure of central tendency (that is, a mean, median, or mode) and a measure of the spread of the distribution around that central tendency (often by means of a standard deviation or quantile).

One such variable is the cholesterol level in humans. For a variety of reasons, you might find it important and interesting to determine the central tendency and the standard deviation of cholesterol in a sample, with the intent of generalizing your findings to a population. We can use an extension of the techniques discussed in earlier chapters to distill data from that sample into a statement of the central tendency and measure of spread for that variable in the sample itself. We can also describe the population itself, to the degree that the sample is an accurate representation of its population.

Certainly, it's true that you do not need to use Bayesian techniques to accomplish this sort of analysis. Frequentist techniques of various types have for decades dealt with just this sort of problem. But Bayesian approaches often provide different perspectives than do frequentist approaches, and those differences and approaches often illuminate in ways that frequentist methods don't.

That said, let's take up the code.

Global Options

The first two statements in the code, both Option statements, tell VBA to

- Start new vectors with 1 as their base element rather than zero.
- Require that all variables be explicitly declared rather than created on the fly simply by using them. I've found through bitter experience that I'm much better off with these option settings than otherwise.

These options apply throughout the code that they initiate.

```
Option Base 1
Option Explicit
```

Local Variables

Then several variables are declared using the Dim (short for *dimension*) statement. And the subroutines or functions, collectively termed *procedures*, that follow these dimension statements can use any variable declared there. Other procedures can specify their own variables, which are declared in the procedure itself and which can be used only in that procedure. This characteristic is often termed the variable's *scope*.

```
Dim MuCount As Integer, SigmaCount As Integer
Dim LowSigma As Double, HighSigma As Double
Dim LowMu As Double, HighMu As Double
Dim MuArray() As Double
Dim SigmaArray() As Double
Dim FactorCombs() As Double
Dim PostProduct() As Double
Dim SumLogLike() As Double
Dim ObservedCounts As Integer
Dim ValCount As Integer
Dim LogLikeMatrix() As Double
```

Specifying the Order of Execution

The first procedure is the Driver subroutine, which in this case simply names the other procedures that are to be executed and provides the order in which to execute them. The user is expected to start things off, whether directly or indirectly, by telling the Driver procedure to run.

I turn off screen updating at the outset. Although the code writes no formulas to the output sheet, you might want to see one formula or more and enter them yourself. Because normal screen updating slows things down considerably due to the need to update any formulas whenever a change occurs on the worksheet, I turn updating off at the start. I turn it back on at the end of the code. Obviously, you can override this behavior if you want.

```
Sub Driver()


Application.ScreenUpdating = False
Mu
Sigma
PopulateFactorArrays
LoadData
LogLike
PostProds
Application.ScreenUpdating = True

End Sub
```

Grid approximations, whether they use one parameter or more, specify the levels of each factor that the grid is intended to represent. So, if an analysis were intended to break down an outcome variable according to the subjects' sex and age range, you might have a design cell for males under or equal to 18, males over 18, females under or equal to 18, females over 18, and so on. Two levels of sex times two levels of age result in four combined levels.

Normal Curves, Mu and Sigma

In this case we want to work with two parameters, termed Mu and Sigma, that are needed to describe a Gaussian distribution, also termed a "normal curve." Notice that the names used for these parameters are Greek letters, the traditional frequentist convention for identifying quantities that summarize their population rather than a sample, and which therefore cannot be calculated directly. (By the time you're finished calculating, the population has changed.)

The idea used here is to break both the Mu parameter and the Sigma parameter down into 100 levels each. Then the code will pair up each Mu value with each Sigma value, creating 10,000 records, each with a unique pair of Mu and Sigma values.

Breaking up the parameters in two levels is easy. The range of values is built into the code, which assigns the value 198.6 as the bottom of the Mu range and 208.6 as its top. Per the previous paragraph, we want both the Mu and the Sigma ranges to have 100 levels each. So for Mu, it's just a matter of dividing the range by the number of levels:

(208.6 – 198.6) / 100

or 0.10, so each range in the Mu parameter is 0.10 apart from its adjacent ranges. The code refers to that distance by the name of `MuIncrement`.

```
Sub Mu()

Dim MuIncrement As Double, i As Integer

LowMu = 198.6
HighMu = 208.6
MuCount = 100

MuIncrement = (HighMu - LowMu) / (MuCount - 1)
```

The code redimensions an array called `MuArray` so that it has `MuCount` rows and two columns. (By convention, the first argument is the number of rows and the second is the number of columns.) Then the code loops through `MuArray`, assigning a subsequent value of Mu to each row in the array's first column.

```
ReDim MuArray(MuCount, 1)
MuArray(1, 1) = LowMu

For i = 2 To MuCount
    MuArray(i, 1) = MuArray(i - 1, 1) + MuIncrement
Next i

End Sub
```

The same process takes place with the Sigma array, but in that case we want Sigma to range across 100 values from a low value of 39.7 to a high value of 41.7. Here's the code:

```
Sub Sigma()

Dim SigmaIncrement As Double
Dim i As Integer

LowSigma = 39.7
HighSigma = 41.7
SigmaCount = 100

SigmaIncrement = (HighSigma - LowSigma) / (SigmaCount - 1)

ReDim SigmaArray(SigmaCount, 1)
SigmaArray(1, 1) = LowSigma

For i = 2 To SigmaCount
    SigmaArray(i, 1) = SigmaArray(i - 1, 1) + SigmaIncrement
Next i
End Sub
```

NOTE: MuArray and SigmaArray each consist of two columns and a few hundred rows. In each case, the array's first column contains the levels of the factor that's specified in the array. Why not declare an array as, for example, SigmaArray(SigmaCount) instead of SigmaArray(SigmaCount, 1)? The reason is that in VBA, when you declare an array with one argument, that first argument in the declaration is interpreted as the array's number of columns in its first and only row.

For consistency, and to avoid driving myself nuts, it's my habit to declare one-dimensional arrays as two-dimensional, with any number of rows and one column. The first argument then shows the number of rows I want the array to contain, and the second argument establishes a column: a valid element of the array that nevertheless forces a particular arrangement of the array's dimensions, so that it causes the first argument to establish rows rather than columns.

If you want to run the code as it is given here, and as it is stored on the publisher's website, you can run it without edits. Or, if the presence of a dummy dimension irks you, simply change, for example, references such as SigmaArray(SigmaCount, 1) to SigmaArray(SigmaCount).

NOTE: If you disagree with me on this point, experiment with one array declared via Dim Horizontal (5) and another declared via Dim Vertical (5,1). Populate both arrays, switch to a worksheet, and choose a range with five rows and one column. Switch back to the VBE, enter Selection = Horizontal() in the Immediate window, and switch back to the worksheet to see what has happened to the selection. Experiment with different combinations of the orientation of the selection (i.e., five columns and one row) and which version of the array to write there.

Visualizing the Arrays

At this point, we have two arrays, named MuArray and SigmaArray, that each contain 100 rows. Each array's first and only column, on each of 100 rows, contains a level for the array's factor. For example, here are the first five rows of the array named MuArray:

198.6
198.7
198.8
198.9
199.0

and here are the first five rows of `SigmaArray`:

39.7
39.7
39.7
39.7
39.7

For convenience in coding and in tracing the code, we want to combine these two arrays into one. When we're done with that task, the first five rows of the resulting two-column, ten-thousand-row array will look like this:

198.6	39.7
198.7	39.7
198.8	39.7
198.9	39.7
199.0	39.7

And the final five rows of the resulting array will look like this:

208.2	41.7
208.3	41.7
208.4	41.7
208.5	41.7
208.6	41.7

Don't lose sight of the purpose of all this. Among other things, we're looking for a combination of the parameter Mu and the parameter Sigma that together produce the optimum value of the outcome variable. In order to do that, we need to associate an observed outcome with the different combinations of the two parameters, Mu and Sigma, and the present code is preparing to make that association.

Combining Mu and Sigma

The following procedure combines `MuArray` with `SigmaArray` into a new array named `FactorCombs`:

```
Sub PopulateFactorArrays()

Dim RowNum As Integer, i As Integer, j As Integer

ValCount = MuCount * SigmaCount
ReDim FactorCombs(ValCount + 1, 2)
RowNum = 1

For i = 1 To SigmaCount
    For j = 1 To MuCount
        FactorCombs(RowNum, 1) = MuArray(j, 1)
        FactorCombs(RowNum, 2) = SigmaArray(i, 1)
        RowNum = RowNum + 1
    Next j
Next i

End Sub
```

The subroutine named `PopulateFactorArrays` makes use of a nested loop. The outer loop cycles through all the levels of the Sigma parameter. Within each level of the Sigma parameter, the inner loop cycles through all the levels of the Mu parameter. (In this case, it doesn't matter which parameter is in the inner loop and which is in the outer.)

We wind up with `MuCount * SigmaCount` rows in `FactorCombs`. Because we called for 100 levels of Mu and 100 levels of Sigma, the `FactorCombs` array contains 10,000 rows, accounting for all the ways that the 100 levels of Mu can be combined with the 100 levels of Sigma.

5   Putting the Data Together

The next procedure, `LoadData`, combines the factor values in `FactorCombs` with the observations saved as a list in a csv or Excel workbook file. The address occupied by the observations is hard-coded as A2:A301. Note that you can replicate this analysis with another data set by adjusting, in the code, the rows and column that contain the observed data and by making the worksheet that contains the data the active sheet before starting the code.

It would be unusual to find a set of observations whose count would divide evenly into the number of combined levels of Mu and Sigma that the code has postulated (10,000). In this case, we have 300 observations and 10,000 combined levels. That means that we can associate those 300 observations with factor levels 33 times, with room for 100 more:

33 * 300 = 9900, and 10,000 − 9900 = 100.

VBA's mod function helps out here. Declare a few variables, including an object variable. The variable `Repeat` will store the number of times that the observed data can be evenly added to a matrix named `LogLikeMatrix`: in this case, that's 33 times, as shown above. The variable `Remain` will store the number of cases left over: in this case that's 100, also as above.

```
Sub LoadData()
Dim Obs As Range
Dim Repeat As Integer, Remain As Integer
Dim i As Integer, j As Integer, k As Integer
```

Now assign the range A2:A301 to the object variable `Obs`. This counts the number of rows in that range to determine the total number of cases in the worksheet range.

```
Set Obs = ActiveSheet.Range(Cells(2, 1), Cells(301, 1))
ObservedCounts = Obs.Rows.Count
```

Redimension the matrix named `LogLikeMatrix` with the total number of factor levels as its number of rows, and with five columns. When you redimension a matrix that you have already declared in the code, and the number of elements in a dimension such as rows or columns is another variable (as it is here using `ValCount` as the number of rows) you must redimension the array. You cannot use, say, `Dim Obs (ValCount)` when, as is usually the case, you have declared an array without specifying its dimensions. It is usually necessary to use the `ReDim` statement, but using it tends to slow execution speed. (There are some other restrictions that apply to the use of `ReDim`.)

```
ReDim LogLikeMatrix(ValCount, 5)
ReDim SumLogLike(ValCount)

Remain = ValCount Mod ObservedCounts
Repeat = (ValCount - Remain) / ObservedCounts
```

Move the contents of the `FactorCombs` array into columns 2 and 3 of `LogLikeMatrix`:

```
For i = 1 To ValCount

    LogLikeMatrix(i, 2) = FactorCombs(i, 1)
    LogLikeMatrix(i, 3) = FactorCombs(i, 2)

Next
```

Now enter the 300 values from `ObservedCounts` into `LogLikeMatrix`. Do so 33 times (that is, the number of times specified by the variable `Repeat`).

```
k = 1
For i = 1 To Repeat
    For j = 1 To ObservedCounts
        LogLikeMatrix(k, 1) = Obs(j)
        k = k + 1
    Next j
Next i
```

Finish populating `LogLikeMatrix` with the remaining 100 data observations:

```
k = 1
For i = Repeat * ObservedCounts + 1 To ValCount
    LogLikeMatrix(i, 1) = Obs(k)
    k = k + 1
Next i

End Sub
```

You now have an array named LogLikeMatrix that contains the observed data set repeated 33 times, plus an additional 100 values from the observed data to fill out the 10,000 rows in LogLikeMatrix. Each value in the observed data set is repeated 33 times in LogLikeMatrix, plus an additional 100 instances of the observed records, which are therefore repeated 34 times.

Calculating the Probabilities

The idea is to calculate the likelihood of each observation across each value of the Mu and the Sigma parameters. This is accomplished by using Excel VBA's NORM_DIST function. The calculations are shown in the code for the LogLike procedure.

```
Sub LogLike()

Dim i As Integer, j As Integer, k As Integer
Dim CurrentMean As Double, CurrentSigma As Double
```

Write the contents of LogLikeMatrix to the output sheet starting in row 2 and occupying columns A, B, and C. This gives you each combination of factor levels and each observed value. Writing out the contents is not a necessary step for the analysis, but I want you to be able to compare the code with its results.

```
Workbooks.Add
ActiveSheet.Name = "Output"

For i = 1 To ValCount
    ActiveSheet.Cells(i + 1, 1) = LogLikeMatrix(i, 1)
    ActiveSheet.Cells(i + 1, 2) = LogLikeMatrix(i, 2)
    ActiveSheet.Cells(i + 1, 3) = LogLikeMatrix(i, 3)
Next i
```

Supply column headers for the output:

```
ActiveSheet.Cells(1, 1) = "Cholesterol"
ActiveSheet.Cells(1, 2) = "Mu"
ActiveSheet.Cells(1, 3) = "Sigma"
ActiveSheet.Cells(1, 4) = "LL"
ActiveSheet.Cells(1, 5) = "Prod"
ActiveSheet.Cells(1, 6) = "Prob"
```

Now the code enters another nested loop. The outer loop runs from 1 to 10,000 (that is, the value of ValCount). The inner loop runs from 1 to 300 (that is, the number of fully observed counts). The idea is to hold constant Mu and Sigma from the current record in LogLikeMatrix—these are the values computed in the PopulateFactorArrays subroutine earlier in the code. For those particular values of Mu and Sigma, the code picks up each of 300 values in the observed data set. The code uses NORM_DIST to calculate the probability of the observed datum given the CurrentMu and CurrentSigma: that is, how far above or below Mu is the observation, in Sigma units? The code then accumulates the log of the resulting probabilities for each observed value in the array named SumLogLike. That array will eventually hold the sum of the logarithms of the record's likelihoods.

> **NOTE** There's nothing especially mysterious about the use of logarithms in conjunction with the probabilities. Something that you get used to in Bayesian analysis is that you're working with very, very small numbers. Frequently, you're working with numbers that are so small the computer cannot distinguish between them, and you wind up with a bunch of zeros. By converting those numbers to their logs you wind up with numbers that can be manipulated arithmetically, including totaling the logs, which is equivalent to multiplying the numbers on which the logs are based. Here we don't need to convert them back via antilogs because what we're really interested in is the relative sizes of the sums of the logs, which is what we have at the end of the next procedure in the guise of products of probabilities.

Notice that in the following loop, we are totaling the logs of each observed probability every time it appears with a different combination of factor levels, defined by `CurrentMean` and `CurrentSigma`. (Bear in mind that there are just 300 observed values, so we expect each to appear 33 times in the expanded grid.) Here is what happens in the nested loops:

1. The outer loop runs through the entire 10,000 records, picking up on the way each record's `CurrentMean` and its `CurrentSigma` from `LogLikeMatrix`.

```
For j = 1 To ValCount
    CurrentMean = LogLikeMatrix(j, 2)
    CurrentSigma = LogLikeMatrix(j, 3)
```

2. The inner loop then runs through the 300 observed records and calculates for each one the probability of observing that record's cholesterol measure, given the `CurrentMean` and `CurrentSigma`. The `False` argument specifies that the probability measure should *not* be cumulative.

Again, totaling the logs is equivalent to multiplying the numbers on which they're based.

```
For i = 1 To ObservedCounts

    LogLikeMatrix(i, 4) = Application.WorksheetFunction.Norm_Dist
    ↪(LogLikeMatrix(i, 1), CurrentMean, CurrentSigma, False)
```

The log of the current probability is taken and is used to increment the running total of the logs for the current observed cholesterol measure.

```
        SumLogLike(j) = SumLogLike(j) + Log(LogLikeMatrix(i, 4))

    Next i
    ActiveSheet.Cells(j + 1, 4) = SumLogLike(j)

Next j
End Sub
```

At the end of the nested loop—and therefore of the procedure—we have a vector of values, one for each of the observed data points. Each value in the vector is the sum of the logs of the probabilities of observing each data point, conditioned on the values of each level of `CurrentMu` and `CurrentSigma`.

Folding in the Prior

We are at the point now where we have a likelihood. We still need a prior so that under the procedures used in grid approximation we can conflate the likelihood with the prior to create a new posterior. I've chosen to use published norms of cholesterol measures to construct the prior. You'll see how that's done using Excel's NORM.DIST function in a procedure that follows shortly, PostProbs.

The prior can be any rational set of values that you want. If you have no idea as to how the prior should be distributed, you could start with a very weak prior, such as a prior that assigns one case to each category in the distribution. Because we have empirically collected data to work with here, we might as well start with that data as our prior. (A weak prior is one whose effect on the posterior is overcome by the much stronger effects of the likelihood.)

> **NOTE** The data comes from a 2013 report by the National Institutes of Health (NIH). The mean and standard deviation of plasma total cholesterol levels were 203.6 and 40.7 mg/dl. An article in the journal *Circulation* reports a correlation of 0.30 between age and total cholesterol level.

```
Sub PostProds()

Dim i As Integer
Dim UniformSigma As Double
Dim PostProbs() As Double
Dim MaxProd As Double

ReDim PostProduct(ValCount)
ReDim PostProbs(ValCount)
UniformSigma = Log(1 / 50)
```

The code just shown begins the process of multiplying the prior by the likelihood to obtain the posterior distribution by declaring and dimensioning several necessary variables. The variable UniformSigma is also declared and calculated to give it a constant value. I'll discuss the use of UniformSigma in more detail shortly.

The code now enters a loop that executes once for every combination we have calculated—so, 10,000 times, or ValCount. The code calculates 10,000 values for the variable named PostProduct. That variable turns out to be the product of the prior and the likelihood. And that, with one small modification, turns out to be the posterior distribution in this analysis.

Each value of PostProduct is a combination of three components:

- SumLogLike(i)

  This is the sum of the logs of the likelihoods of each observed value at the various combinations of MuArray and SigmaArray. These sums are calculated in the procedure named LogLike and constitute the likelihood part of the addition.

```
Log(Application.WorksheetFunction.Norm_Dist (FactorCombs(i, 1), 204, 41, False))
```

This is the value of the prior. It provides the probability of observing a particular cholesterol value (in this case) in a distribution whose mean is 204, whose standard deviation is 41, and which is *not* a cumulative probability but rather is the relative probability of a specific point. Notice that the code adds the log of that probability—the prior—to the current value of SumLogLike—the likelihood, also a log (see below for this operation).

- UniformSigma

This acts much like the beta function discussed in Chapter 3. Its purpose is to scale the probabilities to 1.0, or 100%. Chapter 3 discusses that process in the context of an analysis with just one parameter. In the present case, we can declare a range for Sigma while saving some CPU time. The density of a uniform distribution is given, in R's language, by a function such as dunif (post$sigma , 0 , 50 , TRUE), where Sigma is a posterior value for the standard deviation parameter, and 0 and 50 are the minima and maxima, respectively, that you allow for the prior Sigma. The VBA code calculates the min – max range (here, 50), and supplies its reciprocal (1 / 50).

Its log is taken, so when it's used in the calculation of the likelihood from the prior, you add it instead of multiplying it. Finally, it's an addition of logs (or a product of probabilities) because the code supplies the reciprocal—you add logs to multiply probabilities, and you add the reciprocals of logs to divide them.

Here, we set the prior to a mean of 198.6 and a standard deviation of 41, yielding a different likelihood density for each (unique) combination of factor levels.

```
For i = 1 To ValCount
    PostProduct(i) = SumLogLike(i) +
    ➥Log(Application.WorksheetFunction.Norm_Dist
        ➥(FactorCombs(i, 1), 198.6, 41, False)) + UniformSigma
    ActiveSheet.Cells(i + 1, 5) = PostProduct(i)
Next i
```

Next, the code calculates the maximum value in the PostProduct array (that is, the array of products yielded by multiplying the priors and the likelihoods):

```
MaxProd = WorksheetFunction.Max(PostProduct)
```

Then the code subtracts the maximum value in the PostProduct array from each value in that array, and converts the result from the log scale back to the probability scale using Excel's EXP worksheet function.

The resulting value is not a true density figure but the relative probability for that combination of the outcome value and the pairing of each factor level. It is in that sense a relative posterior probability, arrived at in the log scale by subtracting the maximum product from each product—equivalent to using antilogs to divide the product by the maximum product and then taking the antilog of the result.

5

This process is analogous to dividing each likelihood by the maximum likelihood, but instead of getting a batch of zeroes you get likelihoods expressed as proportions of the maximum product.

```
For i = 1 To ValCount
    PostProbs(i) = Exp(PostProduct(i) - MaxProd)
    ActiveSheet.Cells(i + 1, 6) = PostProbs(i)
Next i

End Sub
```

Inventorying the Results

So, you now have a posterior distribution described by these columns on the output worksheet:

- Cholesterol
- Mu: The unobserved mean of the cholesterol levels in the population.
- Sigma: The unobserved standard deviation of the cholesterol levels in the population.
- LL: The log likelihood of obtaining a particular cholesterol observation in a distribution with a given mean and standard deviation. The value is the total of the log likelihoods for that observation across a given number of sample means and standard deviations.
- Prod: The total of a given observation, the value in the prior for that observation, and the inverse of the constant value for the standard deviation. That total is a logarithm, so using the inverse Exp converts the total to a product on a probability scale (rather than on a logarithmic scale).
- Prob: the probability associated with a given cholesterol level, a level of Mu and a level of Sigma. The values shown are not actual probabilities but are, rather, deviations of the calculated probability from the maximum probability in the data set. This is done to avoid values caused by lack of complete precision in the computer that is used.

Now, what can you do with this data? I'll revert here to R's formula syntax. You could, if you wished, run all the calculations described in this chapter using VBA and Excel, or you could translate them from VBA into R's programming language. Again, I have provided the analysis using VBA and the Excel worksheet because that approach provides a much clearer set of examples than do the R functions. Once you've mastered the rationale I urge you to use R as a much more effective software tool for statistical analysis.

Viewing the Results from Different Perspectives

R has an extensive variety of statistical capabilities that are well suited to Bayesian analysis. You can explore them, if you wish, by saving the output from the analysis provided in this chapter to a csv file, and then using R's read.csv function to pull the resulting data into a data frame, which provides a convenient way to present the data to R's statistical functions.

Suppose that you wanted to find the maximum probability value in the final column of the posterior described here. One way to do so might be as follows:

1. Save the worksheet in csv format with a name such as `grid.csv`.

2. Switch to R.

3. Use **File**, **Change dir** to change the working directory to the location where you saved the csv file.

4. Enter this formula:

```
example <- read.csv("grid.csv")
```

(Remember that R syntax is case sensitive, and many R functions must be entered entirely in lower case.) R not only reads the contents of the file named `grid.csv` but stores the contents in a data frame named, here, `example`.

Now, to get the maximum value found in, say, the `prob` column of the `example` data frame, you could use this function:

```
max(example$prob)
```

which with this data set and this analysis, returns this response:

```
[1] 1
```

which means that 1.0, or 100%, is the maximum probability value found in that variable. Only one instance of that value is found, and that instance is identified as [1]. If you then wanted to locate the full record, you could use this function:

```
which.max(example$prob)
```

and R responds:

```
[1] 9988
```

which tells you that the 9,988th record contains the maximum value of `prob`. That way, you could tell that a particular member of the distribution, with the 9,988th value of Mu and Sigma, has the greatest probability of being observed. Again, just one record has the maximum value and it's identified as [1] in the function's results.

Knowing as you do that the data frame has 10,000 records, you could view the final 15 records (which therefore must include the 9,988th) with this:

```
tail(example,15)
```

Here's a five-record sample of what R would show you:

```
9996    9996 208.1960  41.7 -1545.883 -1554.432 0.9430137
9997    9997 208.2970  41.7 -1545.898 -1554.448 0.9287113
9998    9998 208.3980  41.7 -1545.914 -1554.465 0.9130118
9999    9999 208.4990  41.7 -1545.933 -1554.483 0.8959936
10000  10000 208.6000  41.7 -1545.953 -1554.504 0.8777409
```

Use `head` instead of `tail` to get the first few records.

If you want to visualize a particular variable, one way is with the `curve` function, which draws a particular type of chart. The one shown in Figure 5.1 shows the prior for Mu, based on a random sample of 10,000 records with a mean of 204 and a standard deviation of 41. That curve is overlaid by a calculated normal curve—so, the code to create the chart is as follows:

```
library(rethinking)
random_mu <- rnorm( 10000 , 204, 41 )
random_sigma<-runif(10000, 20,100)
prior_choles <- rnorm( 10000 , random_mu , random_sigma )
dens( prior_choles, norm.comp = TRUE )
title("Random sample of Mu from Prior")
```

A few comments about Figure 5.1:

Figure 5.1
Samples for the Sigma parameter, which has a characteristically skewed right tail.

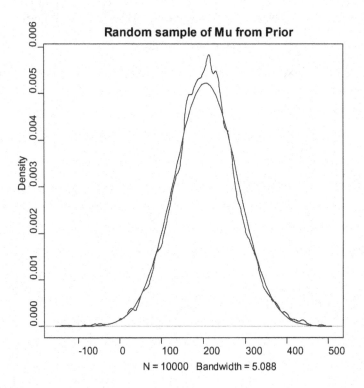

- If you decide to run the code that creates the plot in Figure 5.1, be careful when you run it step by step using the Ctrl+R sequence. That keyboard sequence calls for R to execute the line of code indicated by the flashing I-beam *in the active window*. The problem is that as soon as the line of code that creates the plot executes, the chart becomes the active window, not the window that contains the script. So, if you want to execute the commands one by one, be careful to reactivate the code window before you execute, say, the title command.

- Similarly, if you decide to use the Run all command instead of the Run line or selection command, be sure to activate the script window before you choose Run all. Otherwise, R will not know where to look for the script.

- The N = 10000 entry on the X axis label is self-explanatory: each plot is based on 10,000 records. The Bandwidth entry is a little more complicated. It is a measure of the degree of spread in the data set that is plotted. It's a nonintuitive combination of the standard deviation and the interquartile range.

- The critical reason for plotting a prior at all is to check that your assumptions are consistent with reality. So, if your plot looks like a straight line while you expect a plot of the posterior distribution to resemble the standard normal distribution, it may well be that something's wrong. Of course, all may be fine if you posited a weak prior to begin with—but you have been alerted to the possibility.

- Notice that there are actually two plots in Figure 5.1. One is the slightly jagged one, which represents random samples from a normal distribution with mean 204 and standard deviation 4.1. The other plot is a much smoother one and represents a normal curve, calculated rather than observed. The idea is to give you a touchstone that suggests how accurately, or how poorly, your sample resembles the ideal that you're assuming. You call for that comparison curve by including the norm.comp argument in the dens function.

Not all variables in this type of analysis resemble normal curves. If you move a curve to the right or left on its x axis, the mean rises or falls accordingly. The same is not true of the variance or standard deviation. They are fixed by constraints such as being positive values and constant wherever you move the mean. Figure 5.2 shows Sigma plotted against a range of values for Mu.

Figure 5.2
Density plot for constant standard deviation: Over the range of possible values for the mean, the standard deviation is a constant.

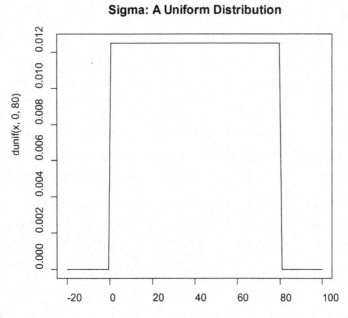

Sigma: A Uniform Distribution

If you're interested in summary statistics, you might want to trot out the `PI` and `precis` functions. Listing 5.1 shows the `precis` function, which provides a quick summary of the variables in your data frame (here named `post`). The code to call for the information is pretty simple, given a data frame such as `post`:

    precis(post)

and R responds with Listing 5.1.

Listing 5.1   Summary statistics for a posterior data frame.

```
'data.frame': 10000 obs. of 5 variables:
          mean   sd     5.5%      94.5%
mu       203.60 2.92   199.11    208.09
sigma     40.70 0.58    39.80     41.60
LL     -1548.19 2.14 -1552.33  -1545.93
prod   -1556.74 2.14 -1560.88  -1554.48
prob       0.32 0.32     0.00      0.90
```

Depending on the hardware and software your computer is running, you might also see miniaturized histograms to the right of the upper confidence level of each variable.

Listing 5.2 shows a univariate statistical inference, based on `PI(post$prob)`. The default interval is 89% rather than the more usual 90% or 95%, apparently due to the developer's distaste for the (largely arbitrary and conventional) limits such as 5% and 95% or 2.5% and 97.5%.

Listing 5.2   Confidence interval for a posterior data frame's probability.

```
5%          94%
0.00149278 0.89731833
```

It's also a good idea to take a look at the posterior distribution of the parameters. One good way to do that is to sample (with replacement) from the posterior, plot the results, and examine them. I switch back to R for that purpose, because R has a slick way for you to control how the sampling takes place.

If you choose to use R to run the analysis I've discussed in this chapter, you'll have the various analytic components in variables that belong to a data frame. That frame might be named something like `Posterior`. Then, among the variables that belong to `Posterior` would be one perhaps named `Probability`. At the point that the VBA code completes, `Probability` plays no role in whether any of the 10,000 records belong with the other 9,999. The code just lined up the first cholesterol record with the first mu and the first sigma records, the second with the second, and so on.

R (but not VBA) has a function that not only samples records from a larger sample (or a population) but selects a record based on its probability of occurrence in the larger sample. You need R to have access to the data frame that this chapter has discussed. If you use R code to construct the data frame, R will automatically have access to it.

If, instead, you use VBA code to construct a data frame, you'll need to arrange for R to pull the data frame into its workspace. The VBA code automatically opens an Excel workbook that contains a single worksheet named Output. That worksheet contains the data frame, which comprises 10,000 rows and 6 columns. Save it as a csv file in R's working directory. You can name the workbook whatever you want when you save it, but for present purposes I will name it `choles output.csv`.

Then, you can use R's `read.csv` function to pull the data into a data frame in R. I'll name that data frame `posterior`.

```
posterior <- read.csv("choles output.csv",header = TRUE)
```

The code then pulls a sample of 10,000 records from the data frame named posterior. This is a 100% sampling, but it's virtually certain that quite a few records will be pulled more than once out of the data frame, and some won't be selected at all. The term for this is *sampling with replacement*. Once you pulled, say, record 123 from the source, you replace it in the source so that it's available subsequently for repeated sampling.

The `replace` argument to the `sample` function specifies that the probability assigned to the record in the main code is to be used as the probability that the record will be sampled. That means that a record with a `prob` value of .0000001 will be much less likely to be sampled than a record with a `prob` value of .0001.

```
sample.rows <- sample(1:nrow(posterior), size=1e4, replace=TRUE ,
    ➥prob=posterior$Prob )
```

The vector named `sample.rows` now contains the index numbers of 10,000 records that have been sampled. We use `samples.rows` as an argument for the `sample` function that actually pulls the records out of the data frame.

```
sample.mu <- posterior$Mu[sample.rows]
hist(sample.mu)
```

Finally, we tell R to show the variable `sample.mu` in a histogram (see Figure 5.3).

Figure 5.3
The distribution of total cholesterol in adults after combining the effects of the prior with the effects of the likelihood.

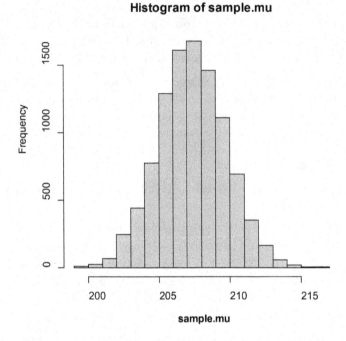

For comparison, Figure 5.4 shows a histogram of the observed cholesterol levels that together make up the likelihood used in this analysis. The addition of likelihood to the analysis clearly pulls the distribution toward a classic normal curve.

Figure 5.4
A slight skewness in the raw cholesterol measures.

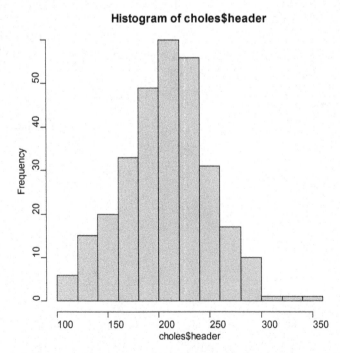

Summary

This chapter has two primary purposes: one is to show how complex the code for a grid approximation can become when you add parameters. The added complexity slows down the processing to a point that analysis loses its effectiveness, and that makes alternative strategies, such as quadratic approximation and MCMC, that much more attractive. I'll be discussing those strategies in the remainder of this book.

The other principal purpose of this chapter is to give you a sense of how approximation and posterior distributions work together. I've always found that the more ways you have to address a problem, the easier it is to solve. There's no better way to get different viewpoints on Bayesian analysis than to compare R against Excel.

5

Regression Using Bayesian Methods

6

Statisticians use the term *regression* pretty loosely.

At its simplest, the term refers to the average of the products of the corresponding z-scores—a.k.a., the Pearson correlation coefficient. At its oldest, the term refers to the tendency of sons' heights to regress toward the mean of their fathers' heights. When applied to categories such as method of transportation, brand of car, or the presence of a defect in a manufactured product, it's usually called *logistic regression*. When particular types of coding schemes are applied to independent variables, which are manipulated by the researcher and not merely observed, it's often termed the *general linear model*. And in a true experimental design, the purpose of regression analysis is not simply to predict but, more typically, to explain. Depending on the context, then, *regression* can imply a variety of statistical and methodological purposes.

Regression à la Bayes

So it shouldn't be at all surprising that the Bayesian approach to regression looks very different from the frequentist approach. Suppose that you want to better understand the relationship between the amount of fat consumed by adults during a year and the amount of low density lipoproteins (LDL) cholesterol found in blood samples from similar adults at the year's end.

Assuming that you have no insurmountable difficulties with the acquisition of good data, you're set up to quantify the relationship between LDL and fat consumption. Just about any application designed to return numeric analyses will provide you with the summary statistics you're after:

- **Correlation coefficient.** A number between −1.0 and +1.0 that expresses the direction and the strength of relationship between two variables. A correlation of 1.0 describes a perfect and positive relationship, such as height in inches with height in centimeters. A correlation of −1.0 describes a perfect negative relationship. An example of a perfect negative relationship is the correlation between the number of correct answers on a test with the number of incorrect answers on that same test.

- **R^2.** The square of the correlation between a predicted variable and one or more predictor variables. I believe that usage calls for the abbreviation to be capitalized (R^2) with more than one predictor, and lowercase (r^2) with just one predictor.

- **Slope or regression coefficient.** The gradient of a line that shows where x-values, such as golf score, connect with predicted y-values, such as years playing golf (see Figure 6.1). You may recall this concept as taught in middle school as "the rise over the run."

Figure 6.1
A regression line slopes up when the correlation is positive, such as calories consumed and weight. It slopes down, as here, when the correlation is negative, such as number of years playing golf and average golf score.

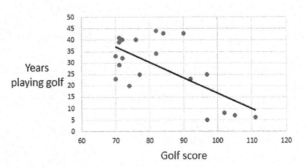

All of the just-named statistics—and more—are returned by any credible statistics package, certainly various packages supplied by R and even the venerable BMD and Lotus 1-2-3. What distinguishes the Bayesian approach to regression analysis is that it does not maximize or minimize the value of some function such as R^2 to arrive at a solution; that is the goal of frequentist approaches. Bayesian methods seek to maximize the probabilities of particular outcomes.

One of the names for frequentist regression is *least squares analysis*. The frequentist algorithms calculate the combination of predictors that minimizes the squared deviations of the observed predictor variable's values from the predicted values. The values of the remaining statistics flow from that finding: R^2, the F ratio, the standard errors of the intercept and the coefficients, the standard error of estimate, and so on.

The least squares approach to regression analysis works with one, two, three, or more predictor variables. Regression's job is to combine those predictors to create a new variable. They are combined by multiplying each predictor by its own coefficient, then summing the products of the predictors and their coefficients. Regression does the heavy lifting when it optimizes those coefficients.

Then, regression calculates the correlation between, on one hand, the observed or outcome variable, and on the other hand, the combined predictor variables. Make one tiny change to the value of one of the predictor variables—say, change it from 5.00 to 5.01—and typically all the other variables change in response: their regression coefficients, the standard errors of the regression coefficients, R^2, the F ratio, the sums of squares—anything except the degrees of freedom.

Figure 6.2 shows an example.

Figure 6.2
The values in the range B2:D6 are identical to those in B8:D12 with one exception: the value in C2 has been changed from 0.4099 to 0.4100 in cell C8. But the regression statistics in F2:H6 are all different from those in F8:H12, with the exception of the degrees of freedom regression.

▲	A	B	C	D	E	F	G	H
		Predicted	Predictor	Predictor				
1		Var	Var 1	Var 2			LINEST function	
2		0.0720444	0.4099454	0.8970701		-0.8552480	0.0435339	0.86527927
3		0.9376171	0.0357070	0.4126903		1.2591799	0.6822929	0.75772504
4		0.3118101	0.0839030	0.7633509		0.2249511	0.4557012	#N/A
5		0.0173270	0.0077816	0.4376309		0.2902411	2.0000000	#N/A
6		0.2831541	0.9347938	0.7263672		0.1205450	0.4153271	#N/A
7								
8		0.0720444	0.4100000	0.8970701		-0.8552467	0.0435292	0.86527935
9		0.9376171	0.0357070	0.4126903		1.2592127	0.6823037	0.75773407
10		0.3118101	0.0839030	0.7633509		0.2249507	0.4557013	#N/A
11		0.0173270	0.0077816	0.4376309		0.2902405	2.0000000	#N/A
12		0.2831541	0.9347938	0.7263672		0.1205448	0.4153273	#N/A

Sample Regression Analysis

To lay the groundwork for a comparison of Bayesian regression analysis with traditional least squares, Figure 6.2 shows the basics of a very small analysis, rendered in Excel. It includes

- Values in B2:D6, which are used as inputs to Excel's LINEST function.

- Values in the range C2:D6, which contains two predictor variables in columns C and D.

- Values in cells B2:B6, which contain a predicted variable.

- The LINEST function, in the range F2:H6, which contains and displays the results of the function. For example, the contents of each cell in F2:H6 are computed with the dynamic formula that's repeated here:

```
=LINEST(B2:B6,C2:D6,,TRUE)
```

6

> **NOTE**
> That formula is known as a *dynamic* array formula in more recent versions of Excel, released in the 2021 timeframe. Earlier versions of Excel use a *legacy* array formula, which requires that the user begin by selecting the entire range to be occupied by the array formula, and to enter the formula via Ctrl+Shift+Enter rather than via Enter alone. One of the results of the changes made to the way that Excel handles formulas is that you can now enter a LINEST formula without either having to begin by selecting the full target range or having to enter the formula via Ctrl+Shift+Enter. If you prefer, you can start by selecting a single cell and end with Enter instead of Ctrl+Shift+Enter. The legacy array formula appears on the worksheet surrounded by curly braces. The dynamic array formula appears on the worksheet without those braces.

■ After entering the formula in F2:H6 of Figure 6.2, I copied and saved it as the result *values* in F8:H12. That is because I want you to be able to use Excel's Solver, or to change the regression coefficients manually, so you can compare the results of that change with the original results. By doing so, you can demonstrate for yourself what happens when you try to maximize regression's accuracy by adjusting the returned coefficients and intercept. (You cannot change just part of an array formula; it's all or nothing at all. But if you have saved the results of LINEST as values, you are free to change any of those values as you please.)

■ The regression equation's predicted value for the first of the five records is shown in cell L2 of Figure 6.3. It is calculated with this equation:

```
=$H$2+$G$2*C2+$F$2*D2
```

which is then copied and pasted into L3:L6 of Figure 6.3.

Figure 6.3
A slight change in the input data or in a regression coefficient can result in a dramatic change in the results.

	B	C	D	E	F	G	H	I	J	K	L
1	Predicted Var	Predictor Var 1	Predictor Var 2		LINEST function				Predicted values		Formulas for predicted values
2	0.072	0.410	0.897		-0.855	0.044	0.865		0.116		0.116
3	0.938	0.036	0.413		1.259	0.682	0.758		0.514		0.514
4	0.312	0.084	0.763		0.225	0.456	#N/A		0.216		0.216
5	0.017	0.008	0.438		0.290	2.000	#N/A		0.491		0.491
6	0.283	0.935	0.726		0.121	0.415	#N/A		0.285		0.285
7											
8					Squared deviations:				0.002		0.002
9									0.180		0.180
10									0.009		0.009
11									0.225		0.225
12									0.000		0.000
13											
14					Sum of squared deviations:				0.415		0.415

> **TIP** You can get the same effect using Excel's TREND function. I used the LINEST approach because I wanted to show the steps explicitly.

- I also entered the formulas in L2:L6 *as values* in J2:J6 by first copying the formulas, and then pasting them into J2:J6, choosing one of the Paste Values options.
- Finally, I entered formulas for the sum of the squared deviations in J8:J12 and L8:L12, and their sums in J14:L14.

Open the Excel workbook for this chapter and activate the worksheet named *Fig 6.3*. Verify that the sums of the squared deviations are both 0.415.

Now, change the value of one or both the regression coefficients in cells F2, G2, or H2. Make your entry a numeric value. Notice that the values displayed in cells J14 and L14 no longer equal one another. While you're at it, you might note that the value in L14 is now larger than the value shown in cell J14.

The value in cell J14 is unchanged from its original value. That's why I saved the results of the LINEST function in F2:H6—so that it would be unaffected by your selection of a different value for the regression coefficient in cell F2, G2, or H2. Either way, the sum of the squared deviations in L14 has increased above its value when the LINEST results were undisturbed. And that means the regression equation is not doing as accurate a job of forecasting outcomes as when you left its coefficients alone.

What's the point of all this? It's that traditional, least squares techniques for regression analysis do not necessarily tell you what you need or want to know about the relationship between an outcome variable and one or more predictor variables. Of course, you don't want to ignore the traditional point estimate that's returned by the traditional R^2 calculations, but neither should you ignore the results of calculations that return an R^2—and associated statistics—that don't quite meet or exceed the criterion of maximized R^2.

To keep some flexibility in your analytic tools, it's a good idea to view the results of a regression analysis through both a frequentist and a Bayesian lens. I've already discussed some of the issues surrounding the frequentist approach in this chapter—in particular, the worksheet function LINEST—so let's now take a look first at regression methods that rely heavily on matrix algebra, and then on one alternative from the Bayesian toolbox, R's quap function.

Matrix Algebra Methods

Suppose that you took regression's job as your own, in a situation that called for you to predict the value of an outcome variable given knowledge of three predictor variables, named *Var 1*, *Var 2*, and *Var 3*. You decide to declare, by fiat, that each predictor variable should be multiplied by a regression coefficient of 1. Then the regression equation would look like this:

```
(1 * Var 1) + (1 * Var 2) + (1 * Var 3) = Predicted variable
```

There is nothing to prevent you from doing that, but it's wildly unlikely that the regression coefficients you chose, a sequence of 1s, will work better than any other coefficients that you might choose. Nevertheless, you will have completed a basic requirement of regression analysis: a sequence of variables, each multiplied by its regression coefficient and added together to create a new, composite variable.

> **NOTE** This is the meaning of the term *multiple* regression. You have multiple predictor variables and one outcome variable. Other kinds of analysis, such as multivariate ANOVA, employ multiple outcome variables. But in the case of regression, the word *multiple* belongs to the predictor variables, not the predicted variable. This leads to confusion in many basic to intermediate statistics classes.

For years, statistical packages such as Systat, and even more generalized applications such as Excel, used matrix algebra to solve regression's normal equations. These processes failed to operate successfully when they were presented with data sets that involved severe multicollinearity. Multicollinearity comes about when two or more predictor variables in a regression equation are strongly or even perfectly correlated.

When this situation occurs, it can throw the results of the matrix algebra off course. Taking apart the matrix components of a multiple regression, you find that the process involves calculating the sums of squares and cross products matrix (SSCP). Then the inverse of the SSCP is calculated. If the values of one of the fields in the original data matrix is a linear function of another one of those fields, then the inverse of the SSCP cannot be calculated. (This is usually because the determinant of the SSCP is zero.)

This problem was known in the waning years of the previous century, but it went unfixed, largely because it took an unusual sequence of events for the problem to arise. Furthermore, the user who encountered the problem got an error warning, sometimes in the form of a lengthy text message, sometimes in the form such as Excel's #NUM! cell value. So an opportunity existed for the user to recognize that an infrequent error had occurred, and to fix it in the data file.

But users did not like knowing of a remaining problem, however unusual, in their software, so developers applied an approach called *QR decomposition* in place of the existing matrix algebra. It's the approach that you find in Excel and other numeric analysis packages even as late as this book's publication in 2022.

However, QR decomposition does not truly fix the multicollinearity problem, which is not a strictly either/or situation. When one field is a nearly perfect linear function of another, problems can arise with rounding errors, and those errors can reduce the accuracy of the analysis results.

Some software publishers have adopted the reasonable solution of displaying a zero instead of a calculated regression coefficient when QR decomposition detects the presence of multicollinearity. This has the effect—possibly useful, possibly disastrous—of eliminating the associated field from the regression equation. Depending on the nature of the linear function, the regression software might set both the regression coefficient and its standard error to zero.

For the time being, though, let's shift our attention to some of the critical elements of the quap function.

Understanding quap

R's quap function occupies a position between the simpler (but often awkward) grid approximation and the more sophisticated (but often murky) MCMC. We might as well begin with the function's name: quap is an abbreviation of *qu*adratic *ap*proximation. (The functionality is also referred to as *Laplace approximation*.)

Behind the scenes, the software makes an *approximation* of the posterior distribution density (the product of the priors and the observations) of the parameter we want to know about; for example, a regression coefficient in a multiple regression equation. To do so, the software uses a *quadratic* function; hence the term *quadratic approximation*.

The quap function is capable of returning a variety of analyses that support Bayesian methods. However, its principal purpose is to build a posterior distribution from samples that conform to requirements that you supply. These often include the location and spread of Gaussian distributions from which priors are assembled. Another purpose that the quap function serves is to define the relationships among the variables in your analysis.

Let's take a look at how those processes might support a quap function that supports the Bayesian version of simple (that is, single-predictor) regression analysis. We start with a little housekeeping:

```
library(rethinking)
setwd("C:/Users/Smith/Documents")
PropTaxes <- read.csv("Assessments.csv")
```

The quap function is part of the rethinking package, so begin by loading rethinking. You'll need to install rethinking first, if you haven't done so already.

You don't need to set the working directory by means of the setwd function if your data file is already stored there; otherwise, use setwd to point R in the right direction, or copy the file into the current working directory.

The third line of R code above assumes that your data is in a csv file named Assessments. csv, so read the data into R's workspace from that file and assign it the name PropTaxes. Keep in mind that the read.csv function results in a data frame, so you now have a data frame named PropTaxes. (Don't forget that names in R, including file names, are case sensitive.)

6

Here's the next line in the R code:

```
MeanValue <- mean(PropTaxes$Value)
```

This statement establishes a new variable named `MeanValue` from the variable named `Value`. It is the arithmetic mean of the variable for all the cases in the `PropTaxes` data frame. The code goes on to subtract that mean value from each observed value, changing the nature of the variable from a raw observation to a mean-corrected value. At that point, `MeanValue` is no longer an assessment measured in dollars but a deviation from the mean assessment, measured in dollars. There are some good analytic reasons to shift the meaning of the `Value` variable in this way, but the principal purpose here is to clarify the meaning of the resulting regression coefficient.

We'll take a look at that shortly. In the meantime, notice that when the `setwd` function creates the new data frame from the `Assessments.csv` data file, it attaches the `Value` field as a variable. You can address that variable directly by providing the data frame's name, followed by the dollar sign `$`, followed by the variable's name. For example:

```
PropTaxes$Value
```

Housekeeping's over, and now it's time to build the model for the analysis. The first step is to name the model, which here will have the name `AssessModel`. The specifications that follow the function name in the code will be used to structure `AssessModel`. Those specifications are assigned to the model by means of the assignment operator, which in R is indicated by the less-than symbol followed by a dash: `<-`. (Sometimes, although rarely, the equal sign is used instead of `<-`.)

```
AssessModel <- quap(
    alist( . . .
```

Here, the result returned by the `quap` function is saved to a new object (a model) named `AssessModel`. The model is made in the form of a list created by the `alist` function. The elements that belong to the list are formulas and as such might include references to variables and parameters that aren't yet ready for use. For example:

```
Tax ~ dnorm( mu , sigma ) ,
```

This is a *model formula*, and it can be used as a component of the list assembled by the `alist` function. A list created by `alist` has some important differences from a list that results from the `c` or the `list` function; for example, elements of the list are not necessarily evaluated immediately. In the prior example, the value of `Tax` can be read as dependent on the purpose of the `dnorm` function and the parameters `mu` and `sigma`. If we don't yet know what values to use for `mu` and `sigma`, we can't yet evaluate `dnorm` or its results. But no worries: we'll get around to evaluating them shortly.

So, that's the first component of the list. Here's where we left off:

```
Tax ~ dnorm( mu , sigma ) ,
```

That tilde operator is used frequently in `quap` formulas, and its effect can depend on the context. Here, it means roughly that `Tax` will be distributed as a normal curve with `mu` and `sigma` as its parameters. In English, `Tax` depends on the result returned by `dnorm` when it gets `mu` and `sigma` as its arguments.

As I just noted, the code doesn't have those values yet. While waiting for them, let's get a handle on dnorm. That's an abbreviation of *density normal*. It tells R to look in the normal curve and return the density (in this context, density means probability) when values have been assigned to both mu and sigma.

CASE STUDY: INVENTORYING TYPES OF DISTRIBUTION

R provides support for 17 types of distribution (plus several less common ones), including the beta, binomial, chi-squared, F, gamma, log-normal, Poisson, t, and uniform.

Each type of distribution can be accessed to return that distribution's probability, cumulative probability, quantiles, and random values. The first letter of the function denotes the type of information to return. The four letters used are *d, r, p, and q.*

So, for example:

- The letter *d*, prepended to *norm* to produce *dnorm*, returns the probability (density) of the normal distribution at a given x-value.

- Prepending *r* to *binom* returns random numbers from the binomial distribution via *rbinom*.

- The function *pf* returns the cumulative probability from the F distribution.

- The function *qlnorm* returns quantiles from the *log-normal* distribution.

Continuing the Code

The R statement that I was about to discuss before introducing the topic of R's distributional function syntax is

```
Tax ~ dnorm( mu , sigma ) ,
```

That statement establishes that Tax comprises the parameters mu and sigma, but we don't yet know how they are involved. For all we know, Tax could be the sum of mu and sigma, or their difference, or their ratio—it's just too soon to know. But we do know that you can specify the normal, Gaussian distribution with only two parameters:

- The mean of the distribution, usually termed *mu*. The mu parameter locates the distribution along the horizontal axis. So, the mean of a population's IQ scores might be 100; the mean of a population's HDL cholesterol score might be 65 mg/dl. It is the normal curve's central tendency.

- The standard deviation of the distribution, usually termed *sigma*. In a Gaussian distribution, about 34% of the cases fall between the mean and one sigma above the mean, and another below it; another 13.6% falls between one and two sigmas above (and another below) the mean; and 2.1% falls three sigmas above and below the mean. It's a measure of the distribution's spread: the width of the distribution, relative to its height.

Software that actually performs Bayesian statistical analysis needs some way of knowing what the underlying distributions look like, and the arguments to the quap function in R provide that capability. Because the Gaussian distribution requires so little information to structure—that is, the mean and the standard deviation—it's straightforward to code.

Furthermore, many topics of interest to all life forms follow the template of a standard normal distribution, and they do so intrinsically. Consequently it's not usually necessary to provide code that takes into account anomalous distributions, such as bimodal curves, highly skewed shapes, and fits that require some grappling.

A Full Example

Let's put some meat on these bones. Suppose that you're interested in the relationship between body weight and LDL cholesterol levels. You have a simple, straightforward hypothesis that, other things being equal, there is a direct relationship between a person's body weight and his or her LDL level. To take advantage of the tools that quap gives you, you'll need an alist, one that looks something like the following code:

```
library(rethinking)
adult.weight <- read.csv("Sample Weight Data.csv")
```

The read.csv statement attempts to open the file named Sample Weight Data.csv in the working directory. You can include the file's path in the argument to read.csv; if you handle it that way, keep in mind that R uses forward slashes, not back slashes, to delimit folder names in file addresses. Or, you could save the data file in what you know to be R's current working directory.

```
sample.mean.wt <- mean(adult.weight$Weight)
  ldl.model <- quap(
    alist(
      LDL ~ dnorm( mu , st.dev.wt ) ,
      mu <- alpha + beta *( adult.weight$Weight - sample.mean.wt ) ,
```

I have given these two variables in mu's definition the names of alpha and beta, because that's how they are normally referred to in the literature on simple (i.e., not multiple: only one predictor) regression: alpha is the intercept and beta is the regression coefficient.

Now we need to establish the central tendency and the spread of the alpha and beta priors. We can tell quap that alpha, the equation's intercept, has a mean of 20 and a standard deviation of 20:

```
alpha ~ dnorm( 20 , 20 ) ,
```

and that beta, the regression coefficient, has a mean of 0 and a standard deviation of 1:

```
beta ~ dnorm( 0 , 1 ) ,
```

and that the standard deviation of body weight follows a uniform distribution with a mean of 0 and its own standard deviation of 50:

```
      st.dev.wt ~ dunif( 0 , 50 )
    ) , data = adult.weight)
precis(ldl.model)
```

And you'll need a set of observations that are stored in the csv file `Sample Weight Data.csv`. They are temporarily stored by R in the structure named `adult.weight`. Here are the first few observations in `adult.weight`. Note that the first row of the csv file contains field names. The `read.csv`'s header argument is set to `True` when the table's first row contains one fewer field name than the table's number of columns. (This is often true when the first column contains row numbers but is not the case here.)

Weight	LDL
165	37
118	48
114	61
117	55
108	33

And here are the results of running the code, shown in `precis` form:

> precis(ldl.model)

	mean	sd	5.50%	94.50%
alpha	58.27	1.63	55.6	60.8
beta	0.06	0.07	-0.03	0.2
st.dev.wt	11.53	1.16	9.68	13.38

You can compare R's results to Excel's by running `LINEST`. The `LINEST` function (entered normally in current Excel versions, by selecting a single cell and using Enter rather than Ctrl+Shift+Enter) is

```
=LINEST(B2:B51,A2:A51-AVERAGE(A2:A51),,TRUE)
```

Here are the results of running the Excel `LINEST` function:

0.064249	58.52
0.070996	1.655082
0.016775	11.7032
0.818952	48.0
112.1677	6574.312

The `LINEST` results require some mapping:

- The value in `LINEST`'s first row and rightmost column (here, 58.52) is always the equation's intercept. Notice that the `quap` model returns a value of 58.27 (second row, second column of the `precis` summary). The two values are quite close, and the difference is easily attributable to sampling error in the `quap` model.

■ The value in LINEST's first row and leftmost column (here, 0.064) is always the final regression coefficient. In this case, because we have called for one coefficient only, it is also the equation's first and only coefficient.

■ The value in LINEST's second row and rightmost column (here, 1.655) is the standard error of the intercept. It is always in that cell, of LINEST's results, directly below the intercept. Its value is quite close to that returned by precis in its third column, second row, 1.63.

■ The value in LINEST's second row and leftmost column (here, 0.071) is the standard error of the regression coefficient. Values in the second row of LINEST results are always the standard error of the statistic in the same column, first row.

■ The value in LINEST's third row and rightmost column (here, 11.7) is the standard error of estimate, and it is quite close to the precis estimate of 11.53. Suppose that you took all the observations at a given value of the predictor and found the standard deviation of the difference between their actual and the predicted values on the predicted variable. That's the standard error of estimate, and it helps you decide whether the prediction equation is more accurate at some levels of the predictor than at others.

Compare the results of the regression analysis as returned by Excel with those returned by quap via precis. It's clear that where the two approaches return the same analyses (e.g., intercepts, coefficients, standard errors), the Bayesian approach and the frequentist approach are either identical or very nearly so.

And you can get those results without risking the slippery slope of multicollinearity. Which makes this a good point to go further into multiple regression.

Designing the Multiple Regression

Suppose that you have data on 50 cars, including each car's weight in pounds, mean speed at which it has been driven, and mean miles per gallon (MPG). You're interested in the effect that a car's weight and average speed have on the miles per gallon of fuel that the car achieves.

One way to approach the problem is with one analysis using Weight as the sole predictor variable and another using Speed as the sole predictor. You could choose the analysis that returns the greater R^2 value as the one to use in assessing a car's predicted MPG.

One problem with running and comparing the two analyses is that the two predictor variables, Speed and Weight, might not be independent of one another; that is, they might be correlated and therefore share variance. In that case, you can't tell how much of the shared variance is shared by Speed and MPG and how much is shared by Weight and MPG. But it's very likely that running two analyses and summing the R^2 values will double count some amount of the variance (because it's shared by the two predictor variables) and therefore mislead you as to the strength of the relationships.

Only in the limiting cases in which the predictor variables share no variance with one another (so they're independent) or in which they're perfectly correlated (so they share all their own variance) can you tell what's going on. Of course, that sort of complete independence or dependence appears only in samples handed out in stats class. (An exception occurs when regression is used in preference to the analysis of variance and the categorical predictor variables are designed to be independent of one another.)

Whether your primary interest is in the total variance in the outcome variable that's associated with variance in both the predictor variables, or the total amount that's shared with each of the predictors, you're going to need to arrange things to combine the predictors without double counting the variance shared with the outcome. Multiple regression does that for you, whether by means of matrix algebra or by means of QR decomposition, and I wouldn't have spent so much ink on the topic if Bayesian methods didn't do it too.

Arranging a Bayesian Multiple Regression

Earlier in this chapter I described how to provide arguments to a `quap` function that support a single-predictor regression. I'll review it briefly here. You supply these arguments:

- A variable that represents the outcome for each case, such as a car's MPG, usually the name of the outcome variable. For example:

```
MPG <- dnorm ( mu, sigma)
```

  specifies that MPG's density is normally distributed (`dnorm`) with a mean of `mu` and a standard deviation of `sigma`. This outcome variable is usually input in a data frame along with the predictor (see below).

- A parameter, often but not necessarily termed `mu`, that represents the result of the regression equation. For example:

```
mu <- alpha + beta ( predictor )
```

- Parameters, usually but not necessarily named `alpha` and `beta`, that represent the constant (or the intercept) and the coefficient (or the slope) in the regression equation.

- A parameter, often but not necessarily termed *sigma*, which represents the standard deviation of the outcome variable. This determines the spread of the outcome variable's distribution across its x-axis.

- A data frame that contains, at a minimum, the values for the outcome variable (in this example, `MPG`) and for a predictor variable such as `Speed`. The data frame might be named `CarData`.

6

Here's how the `quap` function might appear for an analysis of MPG given a single predictor variable, Speed:

```
CarQuap <- quap(
        alist(
                MPG ~ dnorm ( mu, sigma )
                mu <- alpha + beta ( Speed )
                alpha ~ dnorm ( 0, 1 )
                beta ~ dnorm ( 0, 1 )
                sigma ~ dexp (1)
        ), data = CarData )
```

A few comments about the arguments to the `quap` function:

- As I mentioned earlier in this chapter, it's usually a good idea to standardize the values that you supply for the outcome variable and the predictor variable(s) before passing them along to `quap`. Doing so minimizes the effects that numeric overflows can have on the results of the analysis. You can use an R function, `standardize`, to handle this for you, or you can subtract the mean value of a variable from each actual value and divide each result by the variable's standard deviation. (The results are often termed *z-scores*.)

- One result of this standardization is that the z-scores will have a mean of 0 and a standard deviation of 1. It often works out well, especially if you have standardized the predictors and the outcome variable, to use 0 and 1 as the mean and sigma of the `dnorm` arguments that describe the distributions of `alpha` and `beta`.

- Notice the use of the tilde instead of an assignment operator in several lines of the `quap` code. This simply indicates that a parameter is to be distributed as the density of, in this case, a normal curve.

- In this example, `sigma` is specified as `sigma ~ dexp(1)`. The `dexp` function returns the density of the exponential distribution, which is the parent for a variety of other continuous distributions such as the Gaussian-normal, the Gamma, the Poisson, and the Binomial.

  The exponential distribution has one parameter, rate (or lambda); by contrast, the Gaussian distribution has two: the mean and the standard deviation. In R syntax, the exponential distribution's rate parameter is 1 by default, and the `dexp` function returns the density probability for the associated quantile, x (or 1 as here). Among other reasons, the exponential distribution is handy for specifying sigma, because the exponential is constrained to positive returns, and the standard deviation is, by definition, a positive quantity.

That's all you need for a simple regression of one outcome variable on one predictor. To add a predictor and analyze the simultaneous effect of two on one outcome variable, you need four items omitted from the single-predictor analysis:

1. The additional predictor named Weight should be added to the input data frame named CarData above.

2. The additional regression coefficient, for `Weight`, must be specified by the addition of this line of code:

```
Weight_beta ~ dnorm ( 0, 1 )
```

3. In addition, for clarity it makes sense to edit the existing specification for the `Speed` coefficient to this:

```
Speed_beta ~ dnorm ( 0, 1 )
```

4. The `Weight` predictor and its coefficient should be added to the regression equation. In the single-variable example, that equation looks like this:

```
mu <- alpha + beta ( Speed )
```

In the two-variable example the equation looks like this:

```
mu <- alpha + Speed_beta ( Speed ) + Weight_beta (Weight)
```

The full code example might look like this:

```
library(rethinking)
setwd("C:/Users/conra/Documents/Pearson Bayes/Drafts/Ch 6")
CarDataFrame <- read.csv("Cars.csv")
#You may need to adjust the path to the .csv file on your computer
#The three variables are named Spd, Wt and Mileage
#in the csv file. They are saved as newly standardized data
#with new names (Speed, Weight, and MPG) in the
#same steps that standardize them.
CarDataFrame$Speed <- standardize( CarDataFrame$Spd )
CarDataFrame$Weight <- standardize( CarDataFrame$Wt )
CarDataFrame$MPG <- standardize( CarDataFrame$Mileage )
regmodel <- quap(
alist(
MPG ~ dnorm( mu , sigma ) ,
mu <- a + ( Speed_beta * Speed ) + ( Weight_beta * Weight ) ,
a ~ dnorm( 0 , 1 ) ,
Weight_beta ~ dnorm ( 0 , 1 ) ,
Speed_beta ~ dnorm ( 0 , 1 ) ,
sigma ~ dexp( 1 )
) , data = CarDataFrame )
```

You can get a smattering of summary information using the rethinking library's `precis` function. Simply supply it with the name of the quap model you just created, and specify the number of significant figures if you wish:

```
precis(regmodel, digits=6)
```

Here's what `precis` returns:

	mean	sd	5.50%	94.50%
a	-1.1E-05	0.131111	-0.20955	0.20953
Weight_beta	-0.30059	0.137421	-0.52021	-0.08096
Speed_beta	-0.01806	0.137417	-0.23768	0.201556
sigma	0.93517	0.092242	0.78775	1.08259

(The 5.50% and 94.50% limits are how the developer of the rethinking package chooses to pro-test the conventional and arbitrary criteria of, for example, 5% and 95% confidence intervals.)

To check your work, consider running a true regression package on the data that this section has analyzed. One convenient way, using continuous predictors and an outcome as here, is to use the lm package. If you do so after running your Bayesian analysis you can take advantage of the data frame you just created. For example, you can get quite a bit of summary information from these two statements, which return the results shown in Figure 6.4:

```
Car_lm <- lm (CarDataFrame$MPG ~ CarDataFrame$Speed + CarDataFrame$Weight)
   summary(Car_lm)
```

Figure 6.4
The lm function performs a traditional multiple regression analysis.

```
> Car_lm <- lm (CarDataFrame$MPG ~ CarDataFrame$Speed + CarDataFrame$Weight)
> summary(Car_lm)

Call:
lm(formula = CarDataFrame$MPG ~ CarDataFrame$Speed + CarDataFrame$Weight)

Residuals:
    Min     1Q Median     3Q    Max
 -1.824 -0.834 -0.139  0.925  1.723

Coefficients:
                       Estimate Std. Error t value Pr(>|t|)
(Intercept)           -3.04e-16   1.38e-01    0.00    1.000
CarDataFrame$Speed    -2.00e-02   1.45e-01   -0.14    0.890
CarDataFrame$Weight   -3.07e-01   1.45e-01   -2.12    0.039 *
```

Notice first that the intercept and coefficients returned by lm are close to the a (alpha) and Speed and Weight (betas) returned by quap and precis, but do not duplicate them precisely. This is largely due to traditional regression's use of the maximum R^2 as its criterion that a solution has been reached.

> **NOTE** In making your comparisons, bear in mind that lm and precis might each display the regression coefficients differently than the other.

Furthermore, lm by default returns only three significant figures, but you can choose the number of digits with quap's `digits` argument. You might want to compare as many as, say, eight digits in the regression coefficients. One way to do so is via the `options` function. For example, these functions:

```
options(digits=4)
coef(Car_lm)
```

return these results:

```
(Intercept)  CarDataFrame$Speed CarDataFrame$Weight
  -3.036e-16         -2.005e-02          -3.066e-01
```

but these functions:

```
options(digits=6)
coef(Car_lm)
```

return these results:

```
(Intercept)  CarDataFrame$Speed CarDataFrame$Weight
 -3.03642e-16        -2.00472e-02        -3.06564e-01
```

(In the latter two examples I've used the coef function instead of the summary function to save space by showing only the coefficients.)

There are lots of ways to specify numeric formats in R. The options statement, just discussed, belongs to R's base functions, whereas the digits specification belongs, among many others, to the quap function. This situation tends to make matters more confused rather than less.

Summary

And that's the main point of this chapter: to clarify the aspects of Bayesian analysis without confusing you with abstruse details such as the physics of sampling in an MCMC context. It's my intention, and I believe the intention of quap's author, Richard McElreath, to provide a steppingstone from an oversimplified discussion of grid approximation to an overcomplex essay on multilevel regression. It's important to understand how and why Bayesian techniques require a definition of your variables' distribution. Then, you're much better placed to also understand the workings of nominal variables and MCMC, the topics of the final two chapters in this book.

6

Handling Nominal Variables

7

In the last few chapters we've spent quite a bit of time on some theoretical and background topics. I think that the time is well spent, because it's difficult to understand how and why Bayesian analysis works without understanding how those topics come into play. But now that we've covered such issues as beta and binomial distributions, as well as the Bayesian versions of simple and multiple regression analysis, it's definitely time to look through the other end of the telescope.

One of the first, if not the very first, inferential techniques that is taught in college-level statistics classes is the *t-test*. The purpose of a fundamental, basic t-test is to determine whether the mean values for two groups, on a continuous variable, are reliably different. (T-tests are not limited, however, to testing a difference between mean values. They can be used, for example, to test the difference between a regression coefficient and zero. But the calculation procedures are very different for means than for regression coefficients.)

A researcher might randomly select a group of women and another group of men and measure the heights of each individual in each group. The researcher could then use a t-test to determine whether the difference in the mean height of the two groups is statistically reliable—that is, if the experiment were repeated, what is the probability that the same outcome would be observed?

Or, a researcher might randomly select two groups of patients to see whether a vaccine has the same impact on males as it does on females, as measured by a count of antibodies. This approach, in which the researcher uses random selection to assign subjects to either a treatment or a no-treatment group, often terms the group assignment as an independent variable and the antibody count as the dependent variable. The hypothesis is that any difference in the groups' antibody count depends on the group assignment, and the groups are otherwise equivalent due to the random assignment.

The t-test makes a few assumptions, and in some cases you can get away with violating them:

■ **Normal distribution.** The t-test assumes that the dependent variable is distributed in the populations as a normal, Gaussian variable. Although this assumption was made when the t-test was under development it turns out to have a negligible effect on the results of the t-test.

■ **Homogeneity of variance.** The variances of the dependent variable are assumed to be equal in the populations. Again, violating this assumption can be regarded as negligible *if* the samples have the same size—that is, if $n_1 = n_2$.

■ **Independence of observations.** This assumption is critically important: Violating it has serious consequences for the accuracy of the probabilities associated with experimental outcomes. You can avoid this sort of error by careful random selection and assignment, as opposed to a "grab" or "convenience" sample of subjects. You want to be confident that one subject's selection and assignment to a given group does not affect another subject's selection and assignment. This can occur if, for example, one of your samples comprised several members of the same family because you selected them as a matter of convenience. Particularly with softer measures such as political attitudes, the married couple Charlie and Susan do not contribute independent observations, and this throws off your estimate of the probabilities. The couple might well respond differently if they were not acquainted.

A further point to keep in mind is that it is important to avoid multiple t-tests. Suppose you randomly select 30 subjects from a population, and then randomly assign those subjects to three separate groups. You then perform three t-tests to see whether zero, one, or two group means differ significantly from the other means at, say, the 0.05 confidence level. Even if you have taken care to ensure the groups' equivalence via random assignment, the tests themselves will not be statistically independent of one another. The probability is greater than 0.05 that the statistical "significance" of at least one of the comparisons will be in error. I discuss this problem in greater detail later in the chapter. (The problem is that each subsequent t-test uses up some of the original probability space, and the t-test has no fully acceptable method of correcting for that. And that's just one more reason to consider a Bayesian approach.)

> **NOTE**
>
> Several procedures have been designed to prevent the problem of unequal variances and group sizes, among them the Scheffe method, Tukey's Honestly Significant Different test, and the Bonferroni and the Newman-Keuls tests. I bring up the multiple t-test method here because it is an apparently sensible test—but not if more than two groups are involved.
>
> Viewed from a Bayesian perspective, multilevel models address these problems using tools such as *partial pooling*, which improves the accuracy of estimates by shifting their positioning. In-depth discussion of these methods is beyond the scope of this book, but the use of nominal variables in linear regression models is well within it.

Using Dummy Coding

The term *dummy coding* usually means that you use 1s and 0s to signify membership, or lack thereof, in the relevant groups. The choice of 1s and 0s is entirely arbitrary as long as it is internally consistent. You could use *omelet* to represent a man, as long as you used it to represent all men in the study.

You might have five Democrats and five Republicans, for example, with the data laid out as in Figure 7.1.

Figure 7.1
The 1s in the Group vector indicate which cases belong to the Republican Party.

	A	B	C	D	E	F	G
1	Outcome variable	Talking points	Group		SUMMARY OUTPUT		
2	1	Republican	1				
3	3	Republican	1		*Regression Statistics*		
4	3	Republican	1		Multiple R	0.045407661	
5	7	Republican	1		R Square	0.002061856	
6	9	Republican	1		Adjusted R Square	-0.122680412	
7	3	Democrat	0		Standard Error	2.459674775	
8	6	Democrat	0		Observations	10	
9	5	Democrat	0				
10	4	Democrat	0				
11	4	Democrat	0				
12							
13						*Coefficients*	*Standard Error*
14	Mean outcome, Republican	4.6			Intercept	4.4	1.1
15	Mean outcome, Democrat	4.4			Group	0.2	1.555634919

Suppose again that you took a random sample of 10 prospective voters from a group of high school students. You have each of them read a list of talking points prepared by two local candidates for a school board race. Dummy coding, as shown in Figure 7.1, is one way to lay out the results of the study for statistical analysis. Using that approach, the five subjects in the range A2:C6 of Figure 7.1 are identified as Republicans by the 1s in column C. The remaining subjects in rows 7 through 11 occupy the range A7:C11.

Still in Figure 7.1, notice the two group means on the outcome variable—perhaps the number of financial contributions made during a single year—shown in cells B14 and B15. The value of the mean for the Democrats, who were assigned 0s in the Group vector, is identical to the intercept shown in cell F14. Also note that the regression coefficient (in this case, the only regression coefficient in the regression equation) is equal to the mean difference between the two groups. The characteristics of regression analysis combined with dummy coding will prove useful when we look at how R does regression with a continuous outcome and nominal independent variables.

Back when people routinely used hand calculators to perform multiple regression, coding systems such as dummy coding and effect coding were popular in part because they made some ancillary computations much easier. For example:

- Note in Figure 7.2 that the group of independent voters is assigned 0s in both columns C and D, which contain the vectors that encode membership preference. If you were to run a multiple regression analysis of the data in Figure 7.2, you would find that the regression equation's intercept is equal to the mean of the group assigned 0s throughout.

- A group's regression coefficient is equal to the difference between the mean of that group and the mean of the group that is assigned 0s throughout.

Other such shortcuts are available from dummy coding and similar schemes, but the use of personal computers, and software that once required mainframes to run, have done away with their necessity.

Notice that the single vector in column C of Figure 7.1 is all that is necessary to identify the membership in each group. That is generally true. With dummy coding, you require as many vectors as you have groups, minus one. For example, compare Figure 7.1 with Figure 7.2, where we need another column to accommodate a third political preference.

Figure 7.2
An additional column is needed when you add another group.

	A	B	C	D	E
			Group vector A	Group vector B	
1	Outcome variable	Talking points			
2		1 Republican	1	0	
3		3 Republican	1	0	
4		3 Republican	1	0	
5		7 Republican	1	0	
6		9 Republican	1	0	
7		3 Democrat	0	1	
8		6 Democrat	0	1	
9		5 Democrat	0	1	
10		4 Democrat	0	1	
11		4 Democrat	0	1	
12		2 Independent	0	0	
13		3 Independent	0	0	
14		11 Independent	0	0	
15		4 Independent	0	0	
16		3 Independent	0	0	
17					
18					
19	Mean outcome, Republican	4.6			
20	Mean outcome, Democrat	4.4			
21	Mean outcome, Independent	4.6			

Notice that the subjects with a political preference for Republicans still have 1s in the original group vector but now have 0s in the new (second) group vector. That second group vector in column D assigns 0s to the Republicans and 1s to the Democrats. But the newly added third political group, Independent, is now assigned 0s in both group columns, C and D.

Notice what happens to the analysis in Figure 7.3 when we run Excel's regression routine on the three-group data in Figure 7.2.

Figure 7.3
The regression results shown are produced by Excel's Data Analysis add-in. For clarity, most of the results have been suppressed.

	A	B	C	D	E	F	G	H
			Group vector A	Group vector B				
1	Outcome variable	Talking points				SUMMARY OUTPUT		
2		1 Republican	1	0				
3		3 Republican	1	0		*Regression Statistics*		
4		3 Republican	1	0		Multiple R	0.036202431	
5		7 Republican	1	0		R Square	0.001310616	
6		9 Republican	1	0		Adjusted R Square	-0.165137615	
7		3 Democrat	0	1		Standard Error	2.909753712	
8		6 Democrat	0	1		Observations	15	
9		5 Democrat	0	1				
10		4 Democrat	0	1				
11		4 Democrat	0	1			Coefficients	Standard Error
12		2 Independent	0	0		Intercept	4.6	1.30128142
13		3 Independent	0	0		Group vector A	0.00	1.840289832
14		11 Independent	0	0		Group vector B	-0.2	1.840289832
15		4 Independent	0	0				
16		3 Independent	0	0				
17								
18								
19	Mean outcome, Republican	4.6						
20	Mean outcome, Democrat	4.4						
21	Mean outcome, Independent	4.6						

Again, and just as in Figure 7.2, the regression equation's intercept (4.6 in cell G12) is identical to the mean of the Independent group, assigned 0s throughout (cell B21).

And the coefficient associated with Group Vector A is 0.0 (cell G13) for Republicans (cells C2:C6). The Republicans' mean is 4.6 (cell B19); so is the mean for Independents (cell B21). The pattern of these equalities, between the group means and the regression statistics, continues as additional factor levels (e.g., Green Party, Socialist Party) are added.

From a frequentist viewpoint, bear in mind that each time a level is added to an existing factor (or another factor, or a covariate), another vector is added to the design matrix. Then the result is that one additional degree of freedom is taken from the residual sum of squares and added to the regression sum of squares. In extreme cases this might cause you to run out of residual degrees of freedom. And at the very least your statistical analysis loses statistical power because the residual mean square will increase for every degree of freedom it loses. But you won't run into this particular problem when you use R and quap.

7

Degrees of Freedom

The concept of degrees of freedom is a complex one. You use degrees of freedom to correct bias in a statistic that provides an estimate of a population value. The value of the degrees of freedom for a statistic is often (by no means always) the number of cases that comprise the statistic, minus 1. I go into a much lengthier discussion of degrees of freedom in *Statistical Analysis: Microsoft Excel 2016*, Que, 2018.

You aren't required to use dummy coding explicitly. If you were, you might substitute 0s and 1s in additional vectors in place of the name of another factor level such as Green or Socialist. Most commercial software, such as SAS, Stata, and SPSS, accepts factor level names as part of their input data and automatically generate the needed vectors and 0s and 1s (including vectors that represent interactions between factors and between factors and covariates).

Historically, commercial software has used the 0 or 1 dummy coding approach (even when it takes place behind the scenes, so that you supply the group labels and the software provides the vectors and codes). However, dummy coding is not the only useful method of coding nominal variables such as sex and political party. For example, *effect coding* uses –1s instead of 0s throughout all vectors for a particular group. The result of this system is that each group's coefficient equals the difference between the group's mean and the grand mean of the dependent variable, hence the term "effect coding": each group's regression coefficient represents the effect of being in that group, vis-à-vis the grand mean. Figures 7.4 and 7.5 exemplify the difference between dummy and effect coding.

Figure 7.4
An example of dummy coding. The two design vectors have 0s only in the range B12:C16.

Notice that the summary regression statistics are identical in the two figures. Changing from dummy coding to effect coding results in no change to R^2, standard error, and associated summary values.

But in Figure 7.4, the coefficient for each vector is equal to the difference between the mean for that vector's group and the mean of the group assigned 0s throughout. So, in Figure 7.4, the coefficient 2.4 in F20 equals 2.4, the difference between 9.6 and 7.2 in cells C19 and C21.

Equivalently, and still in Figure 7.4, the coefficient 4.2 in F21 equals 4.2, the difference between 11.4 and 7.2 in cells C20 and C21. Compare these outcomes with those shown in Figure 7.5.

Figure 7.5
The only change to the data inputs is the change from 0s to −1s in the cases belonging to the third group (compare B12:C16 in Figure 7.4 with Figure 7.5).

	A	B	C	D	E	F
1	Y	X1	X2		SUMMARY OUTPUT	
2	6	1	0			
3	7	1	0		*Regression Statistics*	
4	11	1	0		Multiple R	0.64
5	12	1	0		R Square	0.41
6	12	1	0		Adjusted R Square	0.31
7	11	0	1		Standard Error	2.29
8	9	0	1		Observations	15
9	10	0	1			
10	12	0	1			
11	15	0	1			
12	5	-1	-1			
13	7	-1	-1			
14	8	-1	-1			
15	9	-1	-1			
16	7	-1	-1			
17						
18			*Mean*			*Coefficients*
19		Group 1	9.6		Intercept	9.4
20		Group 2	11.4		X1	0.2
21		Group 3	7.2		X2	2
22		All	9.4			

In Figure 7.5, the coefficient for each vector is equal to the difference between the mean for that vector's group and the grand mean of the outcome variable. So, in Figure 7.5, the coefficient 0.2 in F20 equals 0.2, the difference between 9.6 and 9.4 in cells C19 and C22.

Equivalently, and still in Figure 7.5, the coefficient 2 in F21 equals 2, the difference between 11.4 and 9.4 in cells C20 and C22. Compare these outcomes with those shown in Figure 7.4.

In summary:

■ You can switch between dummy and effect coding without changing any of the summary regression values such as R^2 or the standard error of estimate. Changing the coding scheme does not make the regression equation any more or less precise.

■ You can compare any of the available regression coefficients with another coefficient by using dummy coding and selecting which group is identified by 0s throughout the design matrix.

7

- You can contrast any group mean with the grand mean by using effect coding. For example, in Figure 7.5, the mean of Group 1 is 9.6 and the grand mean is 9.4. The difference between the two means is 0.2, which is also the regression coefficient for Group 1.

Your choice of contrast—a selected group or the grand mean—might be dictated by the type of effect you are calculating in a meta-analysis. Sometimes you want to contrast a treatment group with another specific comparison group, or sometimes you want a contrast with the grand mean. We'll see how this can work out graphically by the end of this chapter.

Supplying Text Labels in Place of Codes

At the outset of this chapter I noted that one of the first inferential statistical techniques taught in higher education classes is the t-test. One typical use of the t-test is to quantify the probability that an experimental outcome for a treatment group differs reliably from the outcome from a group that does not receive the treatment. The comparison can also be made with some hypothesized criterion: for example, "What is the probability that after treatment, a randomly selected group will have a mean cholesterol level below 80?"

A characteristic of the t-test (which the t-test shares with various other inferential techniques such as the analysis of variance) is its use of the *null hypothesis*. Typically, this hypothesis states that nothing happened as a result of an experimental treatment. Your aim, as an experimenter, might be to show that two otherwise equivalent groups, a treatment group and a control group, have very different cholesterol levels at the end of treatment.

You conduct your treatment and find, sure enough, that each group began with a mean cholesterol level of 80 but, at the end of treatment, the treatment group had a mean level of 60 while the comparison group's mean didn't budge. If the null hypothesis is true—if nothing happened as a result of the treatment—is the actual outcome likely enough to reject the null hypothesis?

Put another way, how surprised would you be if a treatment group's mean cholesterol level dropped 20 points while an equivalent group's mean stayed stuck at 80?

The answer to that question is at the heart of statistical theory, at least as promulgated by frequentists. You often hear people summarize the results of experiments such as the one we're discussing in terms like these: "The experiment rejected the null at the 95% confidence level." This terminology lends a spurious air of objectivity to what is an essentially arbitrary decision.

And in fairness, lots of frequentists, including me, object to the confusion of what's arbitrary and what's objective. Let's see how this works, very briefly, in Figure 7.6.

7

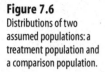

Figure 7.6
Distributions of two assumed populations: a treatment population and a comparison population.

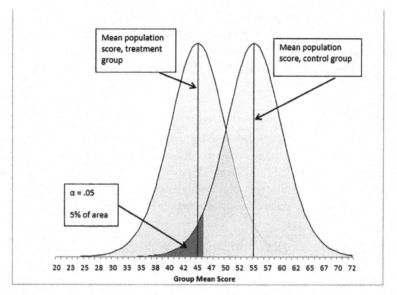

Suppose you acted as a subject in an experiment whose results are depicted in Figure 7.6, and your treatment group exited the experiment with a post-treatment mean score of 42. That would put your group's mean right in the middle of the shaded area in the left leg of the right-hand curve.

Put the results into a frequentist context. If the null hypothesis is true, then there is no difference between the treatment mean and the control mean *in the populations from which the groups were sampled.* Five percent of the means sampled from the control population could fall below 46, even if the treatment had no effect, perhaps due entirely to sampling error, measurement error, or some other source of error. You would be betting against odds of 19 to 1 (5% of the control group shown in Figure 7.6) if you concluded nonetheless that the treatment had *no* effect. If the null hypothesis is true, your risk of a Type I error would be 5%. (A Type I error occurs when you decide that a treatment has an effect when in fact it doesn't. In contrast, a Type II error occurs when you decide a treatment had no effect when in fact it did.)

In Figure 7.6, the point represented by 46 on the horizontal axis is often termed the *critical value.* If the results are as described here, with the actual result falling as it does with respect to the critical value, frequentist logic requires that the researcher reject the null hypothesis of no difference between groups on the outcome variable.

Now, there's nothing especially objective about the decision rules I've just outlined. One researcher might have decided that a 5% rate is too restrictive for this sort of error; that researcher might allow an error rate of, say, 10% when deciding that a Type I error is too likely an outcome. Another researcher might set the Type 1 error rate at 1%. Yet another might decide that 2.5% is just right.

The point is that there is no rock solid, empirically derived principle that we can use as a decision rule for establishing this sort of error rate. There's always some point in the chain of logic that renders the choice subjective, so it's pointless to say of Bayesian approaches, as has occasionally been done, that they're weaker than frequentist approaches because they don't calculate Type I error rates. No one does, at least not objectively.

Contrasting Group Means with `quap`

An issue that is closely related to the probability of Type I errors—that is, deciding that an experimental outcome is due to a treatment effect or to chance—is that of multiple comparisons. Earlier, this chapter discussed the topic of coding in the context of three or more political parties. You might want to investigate whether three (or more) parties would disagree on some political scale or whether two would agree with one another but not with a third.

And which differences can be viewed as "statistically significant"? That is, which differences, if any, can be relied on to show up again if the experiment were replicated with similar subjects under similar conditions? To attempt an answer to that, we need to make multiple comparisons, comparing Republicans to Democrats, Republicans to Independents, and Democrats to Independents.

At the same time, we would like to make probability statements about the group differences, something along the lines of "We can say that Republicans differ, with 99% probability, from Democrats on this issue, but not from Independents." The difficulty here is that with each sequential test, the available probability drops by 5% of the current probability space, as shown in Table 7.1.

Table 7.1   The probability of committing a Type I error increases beyond its nominal value with every additional multiple comparison you run.

Starting Available Probability	Nominal Probability of Rejecting a False Null	Current Probability of Rejecting a True Null
95.0%	95.0%	5.0%
90.3%	95.0%	9.8%
85.7%	95.0%	14.3%
81.5%	95.0%	18.5%
77.4%	95.0%	22.6%
73.5%	95.0%	26.5%
69.8%	95.0%	30.2%
66.3%	95.0%	33.7%

So, with each sequential test, you lose an additional 5% of what's left over from the immediately prior test. If you run all three possible independent party-to-party comparisons for the present example, each comparison may well carry a 5% error rate, but the cumulative rate for the three comparisons will be 14% (that is, 100% − 86%), not the 5% that the tables might lead you to expect.

It might not seem like a serious drawback to statistical inference, but it is. Suppose that in reality there was a difference between how men and women respond to a given vaccine. Using either Bayesian or frequentist methods, how could you possibly disentangle the effect of sex from that of the vaccine by running two separate experiments, one comparing men's responses with women's, and another contrasting the vaccine with its absence?

Furthermore, the combined effects of more than one factor can often be studied together, saving expenses that otherwise might have to be committed more than once.

> **NOTE** The analysis of variance (ANOVA) has traditionally been used to cope with one of these problems, that of inflated error rates for multiple comparisons. ANOVA compares multiple combinations of group means, but because it does so with one test only there is no opportunity for error rates to compound the way that they do under multiple t-tests. However, although ANOVA tells you whether there is a group mean difference somewhere, it doesn't tell you where to find it.

The frequentist approach to resolving these difficulties has traditionally been to modify the probability of a Type I error or, what's the same thing, altering the width of the pertinent confidence intervals. The Bonferroni correction, for example, divides the overall error rate among the available multiple comparisons.

Certainly, doing so makes it less likely to erroneously declare a true null hypothesis as false. However, it's also true that doing so reduces the available statistical power—the probability of correctly rejecting a false null hypothesis, also known as rejecting a false negative. So the Bonferroni correction is not an unmixed blessing.

Bayesian techniques take a different approach, often termed *partial pooling*, to deal with this difficulty. First, it's necessary to discuss calculating the means of groups—in effect, associating the means of continuous outcome variables with membership in nominal groups such as treatment versus control, male versus female, or survives versus fails to survive.

Treating a Grouping Variable as Categories

Look at Table 7.2, which associates a variable named LDL with one named Weight. We'll use it twice in this chapter, once to review the procedures involved in running simple linear regression in a Bayesian context and once to calculate and compare group means. (I'll adjust the variable names accordingly.)

7

Table 7.2   The X variable can be treated as either a covariate or as a grouping variable.

X	Y
6	1
7	1
11	1
12	1
12	1
11	0
9	0
10	0
12	0
15	0
5	2
7	2
8	2
9	2
7	2

You can tell R to analyze the relationship between the X and the Y variable as if they were both continuous variables. For example, X might represent how conservative a respondent might regard himself on some politically sensitive topic. Then you might treat X as a covariate and regress the Y variable against the X variable. This assumes, among other things, that Y values represented some continuous variable such as dollars contributed to political campaigns. Okay, it's a possible topic, not necessarily a good one.

Here is how Chapter 6 suggests that you might run that regression analysis. The data is in Table 7.2. The R code might be

```
library(rethinking)
setwd("C:/Users/myfiles/Documents/PoliSci")
```

The setwd function specifies the location where you have saved the file shown in Table 7.2. It's not needed if you have saved the data file in R's working directory: that's one of the first places that R will look for it.

> **NOTE**
>
> Keep in mind that in R you might have to use forward slashes instead of backslashes to separate folder names in statements giving the path to a particular file.

```
responses  <- read.csv("three groups as integers.csv")
```

The prior two statements set the file path and the file name, respectively. Of course, you can also use any supported file format besides .csv, such as .R, .RData, or .txt. You might want to include the following str statement just so you can check the file's contents:

```
str(responses)
```

You should get something like this:

```
'data.frame':   15 obs. of  2 variables:
 $ Y: int  6 7 11 12 12 11 9 10 12 15 ...
 $ X: int  1 1 1 1 1 0 0 0 0 0 ...
```

Notice that we haven't told R to do otherwise, so both the X and Y variables are treated as integers. Also, R is treating responses as a data frame: that's the default action for the read.csv function.

```
PoliSciModel <- quap(alist(
```

Assign the results of the quap function to a model named PoliSciModel. Feed quap with the list in alist. The elements that comprise the alist list define (*not* assume, *define*) the distributional and formulaic characteristics of the parameters and the observed data.

```
Y ~ dnorm( mu , sigma ) ,
```

One interpretation of the tilde in this formulation is "is distributed as." The data that make up the observed Y variable come from a normal distribution (dnorm) with mean mu and standard deviation sigma. The "d" in dnorm stands for "density" and represents the relative frequency of an observation of that value from that distribution; that is, from the distribution that has mu as its measure of central tendency and sigma as its standard deviation. For example, *maximum density* is another way of thinking about the mode of a distribution.

```
mu <- a + ( b * X ) ,
```

This is quap's rendition of the classic regression equation, perhaps more easily recognized as

$$Y = a + bX$$

In quap, mu is the predicted value, a is the intercept, b is the regression coefficient, and X is the predictor value.

```
a ~ dnorm( 1 , .2 ) ,
```

The intercept a is defined as normally distributed with a mean of 1 and a standard deviation of .2. These figures could well be based on the history of similar research.

```
b ~ dnorm( -.3 , .2 ) ,
```

The intercept b is defined as normally distributed with a mean of –.3 and a standard deviation of .2.

```
sigma ~ dunif( 0 , 10 )
```

The parameter sigma is distributed as a uniform distribution with a mean of 0 and a standard deviation of 10. The standard deviation (and its parent, the variance, for that matter) is constrained to be positive or zero. It is taken to be constant across the range of values for mu.

```
) , data = responses )
```

The data frame responses is the source of the data values Y and X.

The definition of the model provided by quap ends here, and the function precis is called to calculate the posterior distribution based on the priors from quap as well as the observed data from responses.

```
precis( PoliSciModel )
```

Here are the summary results provided by precis, for the data given in Table 7.2 and the distributional characteristics given in the code cited above:

	mean	sd	5.50%	94.50%
a	1.06	0.20	0.74	1.38
b	-0.24	0.20	-0.56	0.08
sigma	8.97	1.66	6.32	11.62

Try standardizing the Y values by subtracting the grand mean and dividing the result by the overall standard deviation. Then run a simple linear regression routine from a package such as R or Excel or Stata, and compare the results as returned by precis. You'll find that the mean and sd returned by precis for the a and b parameters are quite close to the values returned by the standard regression.

Here's the full code:

```
library(rethinking)
#Tne next line must supply the right path to the csv file
setwd("C:/Users/Documents/Pearson Edits/Ch 7/Ch 7 examples")
responses  <- read.csv("three groups as integers.csv")
str(responses)
responses$Ystd <- standardize( responses$Y )
PoliSciModel <- quap(alist(
Y ~ dnorm( mu , sigma ) ,
mu <- a + ( b * X ) ,
a ~ dnorm( 1 , .2 ) ,
b ~ dnorm( -.3 , .2 ) ,
sigma ~ dunif( 0 , 10 )
) , data = responses )
precis( PoliSciModel )
```

Comparing Group Means

Depending on how you obtained the data and the use you intend to put it to, you might want to treat the X values in Table 7.2 as belonging to three groups, which the table labels as Y. From a purely descriptive viewpoint, you might want to calculate the mean of the five X values that are associated with a Y value of 0, those that are associated with a Y value of 1, and those associated with a Y value of 2.

With those three means in hand, you might want to know which is the largest and which the smallest. Moving closer to inferential thinking, you might want to know the degree to which the standard deviations (or the ranges) of the three groups overlap one another. If there is considerable overlap, it's possible that the three groups actually share the same mean value, and any differences among the observed means are due solely to sampling error.

The changes required for the R code aren't extensive. Here they are:

```
library(rethinking)
setwd("C:/Users/Documents/Pearson/Drafts/Ch 7/Chap 7 section material")
d <- data.frame(read.csv("Party codes.csv"))
```

The only change I've made to the first three statements is the name of the data file. It is typical to supply a label rather than a label's code in data files, and to maintain a semblance to reality I have associated, in the file `Party codes.csv`, party names in place of codes 1, 2, and 3.

```
d$Party <- as.factor(d$Party)
d$Party_id <- as.integer( d$Party )
```

The prior two statements have been added to modify a variable and create a new one. The `Party` variable started life as a character (Republican, Democrat, Independent) variable, but the `as.factor` function gives it the intelligence that we expect of a factor.

The `as.integer` function creates a new variable that has a unique integer value for each unique character value in the `Party` variable. So, in this case, a `Party` value of `Democrat` has the `Party_id` value of 1, `Independent` has the value of 2, and `Republican` has value of 3. The `as.integer` function has various applications, but here it is used principally to trace which factor value is which in the resulting precis table and chart.

Then `quap` is used to assemble a model that I've called `PartyModel`. The `alist` function calls out the needed parameters and variables on `quap`'s behalf:

```
PartyModel <- quap(alist(
         d$Rating ~ dnorm( mu , sigma ),
```

The `Rating` variable, which belongs to the `d` data frame, belongs to a Gaussian distribution with central tendency `mu` and standard deviation `sigma`.

In contrast with the use of the parameter a in this chapter's simple regression example, here a assumes a different value depending on which level of the factor is being analyzed. In the regression example, we used only one intercept (and one regression coefficient). Here, we allow the a and `sigma` parameters to vary as the `Party_id` changes from 1 to 3—notice the index `[Party_id]` changes from 0 to 2—and `sigma` is distributed in the exponential distribution as in Chapter 6's example.

```
     mu <- a[Party_id],
     a[Party_id] ~ dnorm( 9.4 , 3 ),
     sigma ~ dexp( 1 )
) , data=d )
```

A vector for a chart's vertical axis labels is established by conflating the `Party_id` and the party name:

```
labels <- paste( "a[" , 1:3 , "]:" , levels(d$Party) , sep="" )
```

Preparations for a chart are made, calling on both the `plot` and the `precis` functions. The preparations specify the model to be used (here, `PartyModel`) as well as two arguments we haven't used before, `depth` and `pars`:

```
plot( precis( PartyModel , depth=2 , pars="a" ) , labels=labels
  ,xlab="expected Rating " )
```

7

- When the `depth` argument to `precis` is set equal to 2, as here, it displays all the model's parameters.

- When the `pars` argument to `precis` is set equal to a character vector, as here, it displays the vector of parameter names.

```
precis( PartyModel , depth=2 , pars = "a" )
```

The `precis` function displays the precis table and the plot function displays the chart. Both are shown in Figures 7.7 and 7.8.

Figure 7.7
The location of the notches in the horizontal bars shows the location of each group's mean.

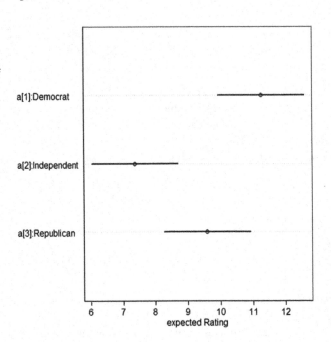

Figure 7.8
The table summarizes each parameter's location.

	mean	sd	5.5%	94.5%
a[1]	11.25	0.83	9.91	12.58
a[2]	7.37	0.83	6.04	8.70
a[3]	9.58	0.83	8.26	10.91

Summary

Next we take up Markov Chain Monte Carlo (MCMC), as well as some of the reasons why MCMC is faster than grid approximation and more flexible than quadratic approximation.

Earlier chapters have shown you how to use Bayesian analysis to replicate ordinary linear regression, in both a simple and a multiple context. This is what the earlier chapters have been leading up to. It's difficult to see why quadratic approximation and MCMC are superior to grid approximation until you have seen some of the reasons why grid approximation can be so clumsy. And it can be difficult to see how MCMC can be faster than quadratic approximation until you have seen how autocorrelation can stick you in some corner of a posterior distribution and take an unreasonably long time to let you out.

And yet, there are times and reasons to use those older algorithms. Sometimes you have only one parameter to worry about. Sometimes you were already convinced that your prior, likelihood, and posterior distributions are each Gaussian.

We can give MCMC its own chapter here. By the time this book gets to your bookcase it will probably have been superseded by something even more modern. But it'll look a lot like MCMC.

7

MCMC Sampling Methods

8

The preceding chapters have stressed that a project involving Bayesian analysis should compare the methods available for generating posterior distributions by means of sampling techniques. This chapter reviews two basic techniques, grid approximation and quadratic approximation, and discusses how a third technique, Markov Chain Monte Carlo (MCMC), improves upon them.

Quick Review of Bayesian Sampling

Frequentist statistical methods such as t-tests and the analysis of variance make use of sampling assumptions, but not in the same fashion as Bayesian methods. A traditional t-test makes three assumptions about two populations:

- The cases in each population follow a normal distribution. This assumption has been shown to be unnecessary: The t-test is *robust* with respect to the violation of the assumption of normality. That's the statistician's way of saying it's no big deal. The t-test can be run on populations that violate the assumption without returning a result that isn't valid. Nevertheless, the assumption stands, largely because the test's development would have been hampered without making it.

- The variances in the two populations are equal. Again, this assumption can be safely ignored *if the test is based on equal sample sizes*. The t-test is robust with respect to violation of the assumption of equal variances with equal sample sizes. (Frequentist theorists have never developed a fully satisfactory means of correcting for violation of this assumption.)

■ The members of the sample are assumed to be—and must be—independent of one another. Brothers and sisters or any other sort of non-independence can upend the probability statements that assume independence of observations (unless special design and analysis arrangements are made, such as the t-test for dependent groups).

Bayesian analysis too makes some assumptions, but none as fundamental as those used by frequentist methods. Instead of assuming that an underlying population has a given shape (normal, binomial, beta, and so on), Bayesian methods generate a distribution of the type that frequentist methods merely assume. Bayesian methods do so by means of efficient sampling techniques. You've seen how grid approximation defines that distribution by specifying its quantiles and how quadratic approximation manages it by randomly selecting values consistent with their probability of occurrence in a given density distribution.

After reviewing the alternatives and how they differ, this chapter examines the method of choice for current sampling approaches, the Hamiltonian Monte Carlo version of MCMC sampling.

Grid Approximation

Grid approximation is a perfectly sound method of generating posterior distributions. But "sound" does not necessarily mean "acceptable." With one or, possibly, two parameters to deal with, and if the parameters do not have a substantial number of values for you to simulate in the posterior distribution, you can simulate the posterior distribution in a flash. But with potentially thousands of cells in a posterior distribution to account for, you probably have a model that's unacceptable for grid approximation.

Suppose that you're designing a new solitaire game, something similar to popular versions such as Klondike or Free Cell. For what seems to be a good reason, you want to know the probability of being dealt exactly four honor cards in the player's hand. At the beginning of play, the player's hand consists of 13 cards, so each hand is a 13-card sample from a 52-card pack, one that is dealt without replacement. This test is run 24 times and the results noted, so you have 24 instances of the number of honor cards dealt to each player's hand.

You can get an answer to your question about the expected number of honor cards using grid approximation: that is, you can approximate those probabilities in a posterior distribution by creating and then analyzing the values in a grid. We've looked at this process in earlier chapters but here is one more brief incarnation:

1. **Establish a grid.** You will need to know how many values the grid will contain, and whether the quantiles will be equidistant (generally they are).

   ```
   grid <- seq( from=0 , to=1 , length.out=24 )
   ```

   This creates a vector, or grid, with 24 available slots but with nothing in those slots yet (column A). (There's nothing magic about the number 24; I simply selected it as one that's neither too small nor too unwieldly.)

2. **Establish a prior.** The prior will normally have as many slots as the grid. In this case, you presumably have very little information at your disposal regarding how cards get

distributed among four hands, and you solve the problem conveniently (if not ideally) by establishing a flat prior. That is, you assign the number 1 to each of the 24 slots in the prior and give the name prior to the result (column B):

```
prior <- rep( 1 , 24 )
```

3. **Establish a likelihood.** Get the likelihood for each slot in grid with the dbinom function (column C). Here's the R code:

```
likely <- dbinom(  4 , size = 13 , prob = grid )
```

Here, the dbinom function is run 24 times, once for each value in the grid. It tells R to return the probability of getting 4 honor cards out of 13 dealt cards, as the probabilities in grid increase in value. The results are stored in a new vector named likely (for *likelihood*).

Here are the calculated values in the vector named likely (see column C in Figure 8.1).

Figure 8.1

Because we are using a flat prior of 1, we get a raw posterior equal to the likelihood.

	A	B	C	D	E
1	Grid	Prior	Likely	Raw posterior	Std posterior
2	0	1.0000	0.0000	0.0000	0.0000
3	0.043478	1.0000	0.0017	0.0017	0.0010
4	0.086957	1.0000	0.0180	0.0180	0.0110
5	0.130435	1.0000	0.0588	0.0588	0.0358
6	0.173913	1.0000	0.1172	0.1172	0.0713
7	0.217391	1.0000	0.1759	0.1759	0.1070
8	0.26087	1.0000	0.2180	0.2180	0.1327
9	0.304348	1.0000	0.2341	0.2341	0.1425
10	0.347826	1.0000	0.2234	0.2234	0.1360
11	0.391304	1.0000	0.1923	0.1923	0.1170
12	0.434783	1.0000	0.1504	0.1504	0.0916
13	0.478261	1.0000	0.1072	0.1072	0.0652
14	0.521739	1.0000	0.0694	0.0694	0.0422
15	0.565217	1.0000	0.0405	0.0405	0.0247
16	0.608696	1.0000	0.0211	0.0211	0.0129
17	0.652174	1.0000	0.0096	0.0096	0.0059
18	0.695652	1.0000	0.0038	0.0038	0.0023
19	0.73913	1.0000	0.0012	0.0012	0.0007
20	0.782609	1.0000	0.0003	0.0003	0.0002
21	0.826087	1.0000	0.0000	0.0000	0.0000

4. **Fold the likelihood in with the prior.** Multiply the corresponding elements of the prior and the likelihood, and store the products in a new vector, here termed raw_posterior (column D).

```
raw_posterior <- likely * prior
```

5. **Standardize the likelihood.** Divide each member of the raw posterior by the sum of all its members (column E).

```
std_posterior <- raw_posterior / sum(raw_posterior)
```

This example is intended primarily as a reminder of what steps are needed to carry out a grid approximation. As such, its purpose is limited. It's what's termed an *analytic* exercise in that the parameter values, combined with density calculations, are used, rather than actual in-the-field observations. For the latter observations, review earlier chapters on grid approximation in this book.

Quadratic Approximation

The second alternative in Bayesian sampling is quadratic approximation. You'll find a couple of examples of this approach to building up a posterior distribution in Chapter 6. Here I'll review quadratic approximation and try to highlight what distinguishes quadratic approximation from both grid approximation and MCMC.

The name *quadratic approximation* deserves some explanation. The approach makes the assumption that the posterior distribution is a normal, Gaussian curve. The logarithms of the values making up that curve closely resemble a parabola. Because a parabola is a quadratic function, it has become customary to refer to the approximation that's based on a parabola as a quadratic approximation.

The assumption that a posterior distribution constitutes a normal curve is a strong one, but it's well founded. Many distributions that occur naturally, such as the height and weight of animals and the temperature and blood pressure of humans, follow normal curves. This characteristic of naturally occurring variables buys us something: it buys us time. In particular, it buys us the time needed to do the sampling that approximates the assumed, normal curve of a posterior distribution.

A normal curve has a variety of useful attributes. Among them are the fact that any true normal curve can be drawn if you have values for its mean and its standard deviation (or spread). You can place the mean by simply finding the value of the mean on the X or horizontal axis.

If you know the standard deviation as well as the mean, you can complete the creation of the entire normal curve. The standard deviation is constant throughout with the curve; that's why it's a *standard* deviation. Your computer applies the relationship between the standard deviation and the amount that the curve drops as you move further and further from the mean. Your computer can use this amount as calculated near the top of the curve to derive this slope at any point on the remainder of the curve.

You can see the time savings that this affords you compared with grid approximation. Using a grid, you must calculate the likelihood for every point in your data set. Given that, you can convert your raw probabilities to first a raw, then a standardized posterior. Your computer can do that for you in a flash if you have only one or two parameters to estimate—say, sex and political party affiliation. But that flash can easily turn into what seems like forever if you have 10 or 20 parameters and 10 or 20 meaningful values of each parameter.

But if all you have to do is (1) assume that the posterior is a normal distribution and (2) tell the computer where to find the priors and the data so that it can calculate means and standard deviations, then forever is going to start to feel more like a flash.

So that's where the quadratic approximation gets its deserved reputation for sampling speed. It's an important step in the right direction, but for years, taking that step required an equally strong assumption: that the posterior distribution constituted a normal curve. This is the sort of thing that Bayesians took some pride in avoiding. The assumption of normal distributions is bedrock frequentist theory. That's so even if, as it turns out, frequentists were violating the assumption all the time and the robustness studies showed that it didn't seem to matter.

One of the reasons that I wanted to discuss all three general approaches (grid approximation, quadratic approximation, and MCMC) to generating a posterior distribution in this final chapter is that all three approaches can return close to the same findings. A priori, it's unlikely that all three would return exactly the same value because they do not use precisely equivalent computations. And yet, the values that they return tend to be very close to one another. So your choice of method should be based on issues such as speed of execution and complexity of design. And after all, speed is an important criterion for choosing a method that will run to completion in a few seconds versus one that is likely to complete overnight.

Let's take a look at an example, one that contrasts grid approximation with quadratic approximation. Figure 8.2 shows the results of a grid approximation in which the grid itself contains exactly 100 slots.

Figure 8.2
Notice that the maximum standardized posterior value in this case is 0.233 and it's associated with a grid probability of 0.320. With these data, the maximum standardized posterior value of 0.233 is attained when the probability of dealing four honors is 0.320.

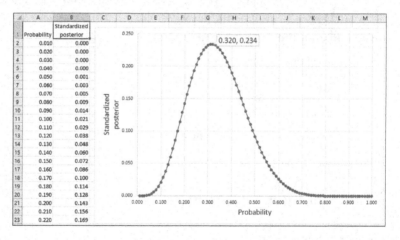

I'll continue with the solitaire card game example discussed earlier in this chapter. In Figure 8.2, I have created a grid that contains 100 levels of probability. I used a flat prior consisting entirely of 1s, so it has no effect when the prior is first multiplied by the likelihood. So column A in the figure consists of the probabilities that I want to see, and column B contains the likelihoods determined by using the dbinom function in conjunction with the 4 wins (4 honor cards) out of 13 cards dealt to the solitaire player.

I put the contents of Figure 8.2 together using Excel rather than R, principally because Excel makes it much more straightforward to show lists such as those in columns A and B along with charts, as shown to the right of columns A and B in Figure 8.2.

The standardized posterior values in Figure 8.2's chart (and in column B) are all calculated using the Excel worksheet function BINOM.DIST. For example, the formula in cell B2 is =BINOM.DIST(4,13,A2,FALSE), and it is copied down to the end of the data in column B.

The chart shows you that the maximum value in the posterior distribution is 0.233. That value is paired with the 0.320 value as the probability of four honors in any given 13-card hand. In other words, the grid approximation tells you that the maximum probability of 0.320 comes about when the maximum value of the posterior distribution is 0.233.

> **NOTE** As always in Bayesian analysis, don't be greatly concerned if you run the same analysis twice and notice very small differences in the two sets of results. This can easily come about because of slight differences in the samples. For example, when I was preparing this example, R returned a posterior distribution of 0.234. On a second trial, R returned a posterior distribution of value of 0.233. I have learned to double check these things and refuse to lose sleep over them.

Now let's take a look at what a quadratic approximation tells us and compare it to the results returned by the grid approximation (see Listing 8.1).

Listing 8.1   Bear in mind that when you are using R's `dbinom` function, you supply wins and losses as arguments, but when you are using the `dbeta` function you supply wins and total trials as arguments.

```
library(rethinking)
cards <- quap(
    alist(
        honors ~ dbinom( honors + plain ,p) ,   # likelihood
        p ~ dunif(0,1)                           # flat prior
    ) ,
    data=list(honors=4, plain=9) )

# summarize quadratic approximation
precis( cards , digits = 5)
    mean      sd      5.5%     94.5%
p 0.30769 0.12801 0.10311 0.51227
```

Listing 8.1 displays all that's necessary to execute a quap function with these data. The quap function is also known as a helper function. It takes the information that you supply to it and translates that information into syntax recognized by R (specifically, by RStan). For example, see the arguments to `alist` in Listing 8.1. In this case you would be telling quap that `honors` follows a binomial distribution with parameters `honors` plus `plain`, and `p`. A couple of lines later, on the `data` line, we tell R that the value of `honors` is 4 (that's four honor cards) and the value of `plain` is 9 (9 plain cards per suit), while `p` is distributed as a uniform prior.

The model that results from these definitions is saved with the name `cards`. The final command in the code assigns the model's results to a table showing the mean of the posterior distribution, which is the maximum value of that distribution. *In this case, that's 0.308, a result which is quite close to the result of 0.320, the value that is returned by grid approximation and the slight degree of error that we come to expect from Bayesian methods.*

MCMC Gets Up To Speed

Quadratic approximation is not a complete solution to the difficulties presented by grid approximation. Quadratic approximation is definitely faster than grid approximation, but that comes with a price. As discussed earlier in this chapter, to use a function such as quap, you have to make the fairly strong assumption that the posterior distribution is normal—that is, Gaussian—and many problems cannot be satisfactorily addressed using software that demands that assumption.

Therefore, statisticians started to experiment with alternatives to quadratic approximation—alternatives that did not impose the straitjacket of normal distributions on their data set or their experimental designs. The methods that they arrived at, collectively termed *Metropolis algorithms*, were much more liberal in their acceptance of other shapes for their posterior distributions. Gibbs sampling is one such method.

However, it turned out that Metropolis algorithms were comparatively slow. The gains that were provided by the ability to deal with other-than-Gaussian posteriors were seriously outweighed by the lengthy time required to complete the analysis of a reasonably detailed design. Two issues tended to cause the problem: *leapfrogging* and *step sizes*. Leapfrogging refers to the number of steps that separate two consecutive data points in the posterior. Step size, of course, refers to the size of each step that makes the path between two points. Certain combinations of leapfrogging and step size tend to cause autocorrelation between consecutive points.

And when those points are autocorrelated, you wind up with lots of points in a particular area of the distribution, and you seem not to get anywhere. The result is that it can seem like forever to fill in any portion of the posterior that is not favored by the autocorrelation between points. MCMC sampling algorithms use what is called a *warmup phase* to choose leapfrog steps and step sizes in such a fashion that the autocorrelation is minimized. You will often see output that details the amount of time spent in that warmup phase as distinct from actual sampling.

A Sample MCMC Analysis

Let's take a look at how you might use the ulam function to analyze a design that contains one factor and an additional variable to put us in a position to examine interaction. The discussion in most of the remainder of this chapter focuses on how interaction can be assessed when the interacting variables are numeric rather than nominal.

I'll use ulam rather than quap in this chapter partly because ulam can execute much faster than quap, even though you are not restricted to quadratic posteriors as you are with quap. You should have the option of running MCMC code when your design calls for it. The ulam function tends to build on the quap function, so although there is some learning to do regarding ulam's capabilities, you need not start from scratch.

I'll use data on 40 patients from two hospitals:

- A 0/1 variable, *Hospital*, that identifies which hospital a patient's data came from—this is the factor in this design.

- Two numeric variables, named *outcome* and *history*, which are factor scores on medical test batteries given to each patient. You can think of Factor 2 as a battery of predictive tests.

> **NOTE**
>
> Statistics has two very different meanings for the term *factor*. One meaning is a variable that expresses a nominal scale; for example, the factor *Car* might have values that include *Ford, Toyota,* and *Nissan*. Your intent might be to compare the average miles per gallon for each of those makes.
>
> Another meaning for the word *factor* is an unobservable characteristic that multivariate techniques employ to combine many observable characteristics into one, or just a very few, variables. The result of that combination is also termed a factor. You can usually tell from the context which meaning is intended. Here, I'm using both.

We would like to determine whether an interaction exists between History and Hospital. You'll find that although most statistics textbooks definitely cover the topic of interaction, they do so only to the extent of interactions between factors, rather than between a factor and a numeric variable. MCMC generally, and Hamiltonian Monte Carlo in particular, are perfectly capable of performing this sort of analysis.

The layout of the data for input to the software is partially shown in Figure 8.3. You'll find a csv file containing all the data on this book's website. (I say "partially" because there is not enough room to show all the cases.)

Figure 8.3

Notice that the value of hospital changes from 1 to 2 at row number 22.

	A	B	C	D
1		outcome	history	hospital
2	1	0.879712	-0.29166	1
3	2	0.75523	0.122564	1
4	3	0.806156	-0.30601	1
5	4	0.810858	-0.30504	1
6	5	1.050743	0.003409	1
7	6	0.827254	-0.42903	1
8	7	0.864425	-0.40694	1
9	8	0.885329	0.13643	1
10	9	0.763789	-0.16041	1
11	10	0.805933	-0.143	1
12	11	0.878097	-0.36744	1
13	12	0.996653	-0.40727	1
14	13	0.885285	-0.39195	1
15	14	1.009434	-0.40001	1
16	15	0.961385	-0.19153	1
17	16	0.800214	-0.39275	1
18	17	0.757871	-0.42113	1
19	18	1.023715	-0.05738	1
20	19	0.885959	-0.40356	1
21	20	0.890997	-0.33213	1
22	50	0.964755	-0.19517	2
23	51	1.16627	0.038144	2

We would like to know whether the regression line between the outcome variable and the predictor variable depends on which hospital the patient occupies. In particular, we would like to know whether the regression lines intercept or their slopes change depending on whether patients are in Hospital 1 or Hospital 2.

There aren't many differences between the user's view of the quap function and the ulam function, but those that exist are important. Interestingly, two of the most important differences you find will come in the nature of advice rather than as an inviolable rule:

■ If you need to make any changes such as log transformations or standardizations such as mean differences, do so in the code prior to invoking the ulam function. You could easily and unintentionally slow things down if you wait to apply your transformations until ulam is working.

■ If you plan to submit data that is at present stored in a data frame, convert that data frame to a list before calling ulam. Here's the rationale: Data frames in R are not permitted to have a different number of records in each variable. A value such as NA might stand in for a missing value on any given record, but that's in the normal course of events.

If the Stan code (which you won't see unless you specifically call for it) encounters an NA value in the data that you pass along to it, the code will respond with an error message (and not a clear one, either) and terminate processing. The recommendation to avoid this situation is for you to supply the data as a list, not as a data frame. The R coding syntax specifically permits NA values when they are part of a list. If you pass along the data as a list, you dodge the problem presented by an NA value in a data frame.

Four different columns contain data in Figure 8.3:

■ Column A contains numbers that serve only to specify which row contains information on which case. They have nothing to do with the analysis itself. Cell A1 typically is left empty in a csv file that you read into an R data frame.

■ Column B, labeled *outcome* in cell B1, contains a set of factor scores on the same patients as in column A. The outcome scores simply represent whether patients had a more or less favorable outcome at the hospital where they were treated.

■ Column C is labeled *history* in cell C1. The data in column C are factor scores for the same patients as shown in columns A and B. The scores result from a factor analysis of patient histories at the two different hospitals.

■ Column D, labeled *hospital* in cell D1, simply indicates whether a patient attended Hospital 1 or Hospital 2.

The question arises as to whether these data indicate that there is an interaction between one predictor variable, History, and the other predictor variable, Hospital. For example, does the regression line between history and outcome vary its slope, or its intercept, according to which hospital a patient attended? It's more typical to see interactions reported between two categorical variables such as sex and political preference. But interactions between a categorical variable and a continuous variable, or between two continuous variables, are by no means rare (they're often tested in the analysis of covariance, for example, for a common regression coefficient). They can be even more important than those between two categorical variables.

Listing 8.2 shows how you might address the question using the `ulam` function. There's not a lot of code involved in this example.

Listing 8.2   `ulam` code as it might appear in R's script window. The code can be found in *Listing 8-2.txt.*

```
library(rethinking)
#Here you'll want to use the setwd function to tell R where on your #computer
to find the csv file with the input data. For example:#setwd ("C:/Users/
Documents/Edits/Ch 8/TestDataSet")
data_in <-read.csv("ulam example.csv")
model <- ulam(
            alist(
                outcome ~ dnorm( mu , sigma ) ,
                mu <- a[hospital] + b[hospital]* history   ,
                a[hospital] ~ dnorm( 1 , 0.1 ) ,
                b[hospital] ~ dnorm( 0 , 0.3 ) ,
                sigma ~ dexp( 1 )
                ) , data=data_in , chains=1 )

    precis( model , depth=2 )
```

The code starts with the `library` command, which in this case loads a library named `rethinking`. This command is needed because later on the code is going to invoke the `ulam` function, and R needs to know where to look for it.

The second line of executable code makes use of the function `setwd`. It's not strictly part of this example, but it's a very useful command nevertheless. I like to keep different projects separate from one another, and when I continue work on a project, its `setwd` function automatically tells R to open and save files to the proper folder.

Then the code reads the csv file shown in Figure 8.3. By default, the function places the data that it reads into an R data frame. That may cause a problem, one that we'll deal with shortly.

> **NOTE** You'll need to alter the path and/or the file name of the csv file in the code so that it matches your own local setup. A sample data file is supplied for this chapter, named *ulam example.csv*, that provides the data for the analyses in Figures 8.4 and 8.6.

Next we arrive at the definition of the model that we're after. I have given the name *model* to the model, and indicated that the model should be generated by the function named ulam. The `alist` function returns a special sort of list in R, one that can take on a variety of argument types. Here, it passes the following along to RStan by way of `ulam`:

- `outcome ~ dnorm( mu , sigma )`

  `outcome` is distributed as the density of the normal distribution, with mean `mu` and standard deviation `sigma`.

- `mu <- a[hospital] + b[hospital]*(history)`

  `mu` is the result of the regression equation, where a is the intercept and b is the coefficient for `history`. The value of `hospital` varies and depends on which hospital is chosen.

- `a[hospital] ~ dnorm( 1 , 0.1 )`

  a, the intercept for each hospital, is distributed as the density of a normal curve, with mean 1 and standard deviation 0.1.

- `b[hospital] ~ dnorm( 0 , 0.3 )`

  b, the regression coefficient for history at each hospital, is distributed as the density of a normal curve, with mean 0 and standard deviation 0.3.

- `sigma ~ dexp( 1 )`

  `sigma` is distributed as the density of the exponential distribution, with mean 1.

You can tell from glancing at the list of the `ulam` arguments that you are in a position to define the shape and distribution family of the parameters: the tilde is used in the definition of `outcome`, `sigma`, a, and b. Using `ulam` rather than `quap`, you need not assume that the posterior distribution constitutes a normal Gaussian curve.

Finally, the `precis` function provides the intercept and the regression coefficient for each of two regression equations (shown as the *mean*) as well as the coefficient's standard error (shown as the *sd*) (see Figure 8.4).

Figure 8.4
The n_eff and Rhat4 tell you how well your sampling is working given your model and data.

	A	B	C	D	E	F	G
1		mean	sd	5.50%	94.50%	n_eff	Rhat4
2	a[1]	0.91	0.04	0.85	0.96	242	1
3	a[2]	1.06	0.02	1.02	1.09	344	1
4	b[1]	0.09	0.12	-0.1	0.28	244	1
5	b[2]	-0.15	0.13	-0.35	0.06	452	1
6	sigma	0.11	0.01	0.09	0.13	372	1

ulam's Output

When you run the `ulam` code as given earlier in this chapter, you will see that it takes somewhat longer for R to deal with the rethinking library than you might expect. On a multicore HP laptop, I might have to wait a little while before I can proceed after executing the `library` command, but the wait time does not strain my patience. Up to the `ulam` function, the code moves very fast. It takes about 30 seconds to run the `ulam` function—that's not out of line.

The output can be lengthier than you might suppose. There is considerable diagnostic information at the outset, well before you get to the summary information provided by the precis function. Figure 8.5 shows you the beginning of what you can expect to see displayed in R's console if you have entered both the data and the code correctly.

Figure 8.5
The warmup phase is time that the Stan code takes to optimize the step size and number of leapfrogs for designing its sampling plan.

```
R Console
SAMPLING FOR MODEL '96395265566a75b373fec0216e2193a3' NOW (CHAIN 1).
Chain 1:
Chain 1: Gradient evaluation took 0 seconds
Chain 1: 1000 transitions using 10 leapfrog steps per transition would take 0 seconds.
Chain 1: Adjust your expectations accordingly!
Chain 1:
Chain 1:
Chain 1: Iteration:    1 / 1000 [  0%]  (Warmup)
Chain 1: Iteration: 100 / 1000 [ 10%]  (Warmup)
Chain 1: Iteration: 200 / 1000 [ 20%]  (Warmup)
Chain 1: Iteration: 300 / 1000 [ 30%]  (Warmup)
Chain 1: Iteration: 400 / 1000 [ 40%]  (Warmup)
Chain 1: Iteration: 500 / 1000 [ 50%]  (Warmup)
Chain 1: Iteration: 501 / 1000 [ 50%]  (Sampling)
Chain 1: Iteration: 600 / 1000 [ 60%]  (Sampling)
Chain 1: Iteration: 700 / 1000 [ 70%]  (Sampling)
Chain 1: Iteration: 800 / 1000 [ 80%]  (Sampling)
Chain 1: Iteration: 900 / 1000 [ 90%]  (Sampling)
Chain 1: Iteration: 1000 / 1000 [100%]  (Sampling)
Chain 1:
Chain 1:  Elapsed Time: 0.045 seconds (Warm-up)
Chain 1:                0.024 seconds (Sampling)
Chain 1:                0.069 seconds (Total)
Chain 1:
```

And referring back to Figure 8.4, it shows you what HMC (or, if you prefer, MCMC) has to say about the empirical issues addressed by the sample study we've discussed here.

As discussed in previous chapters, the precis function returns the most probable values for each variable in the model, as determined by the sampling process. In this case, precis finds the most probable value for, say, a regression coefficient (labeled the *mean* in this example) in the posterior distribution and displays it in the precis table. Again in this example, the precis function also returns the standard error associated with each regression coefficient (labeled the *sd*).

Validating the Results

By comparing the results returned by the ulam function with the results returned by functions that are designed specifically for regression analysis, it's possible to determine the degree to which the Bayesian results agree with frequentist results.

Figure 8.6 shows the results of Excel's LINEST worksheet function, run on the same data used for ulam to produce the results shown in Figure 8.4. I've displayed the results in that way because it's more straightforward to identify specific entries using Excel's row-and-column convention than in an R table. Furthermore, you can compare the results of a traditional analysis in Figure 8.6 with the ulam results in Figure 8.4. The Excel array formulas for the traditional analysis are as follows:

```
=LINEST(B2:B21,C2:D21,,TRUE)
```

and

```
=LINEST(B22:B41,C22:D41,,TRUE)
```

Compare the results shown in Figure 8.4 with those shown in Figure 8.6.

Figure 8.6
LINEST results based
on data from Hospital 1
and Hospital 2.

	A	B	C
1	0	0.038505	0.886857
2	0	0.117458	0.036775
3	0.041733	0.09375	#N/A
4	0.370179	17	#N/A
5	0.006507	0.149413	#N/A
6			
7	0	-0.18024	1.057765
8	0	0.152235	0.025007
9	0.090549	0.111212	#N/A
10	0.846298	17	#N/A
11	0.020934	0.210258	#N/A

The LINEST worksheet function is not designed to return a regression analysis that accounts for multiple intercepts; therefore, it's necessary to run LINEST once for each hospital in the data set. The two sets of LINEST results are shown in A1:C5 and A7:C11 of Figure 8.6. It's not necessary to adopt the same approach when you're analyzing data using ulam because the code provides for an intercept and a regression coefficient for each hospital.

The results of the LINEST analyses are very close to those returned by the ulam function combined with the precis function. For example, compare the values shown in cells B2:C2 of Figure 8.4 with those shown in cells C1:C2 of Figure 8.6. When you do so, you will be comparing LINEST's calculation of the regression coefficient in Hospital 1 (Figure 8.6, cell C1) with ulam's calculation of the same coefficient, also in Hospital 1 (Figure 8.4, cell B2). You can also compare the standard errors of the same two regression coefficients by comparing cell C2 of Figure 8.4 with cell C2 of Figure 8.6.

In each case, the two numbers that you compare are very close to one another, and the minor discrepancies that you find are easily explained by the difference between standard arithmetic and calculus, especially when the calculations are based on sample sizes as few as 20 per sample.

There are three other comparisons that you should make between the results in Figure 8.4 and Figure 8.6:

- Figure 8.4, cells B4 and C4 with Figure 8.6, cells B1 and B2
- Figure 8.4, cells B3 and C3 with Figure 8.6, cells C7 and C8
- Figure 8.4, cells B5 and C5 with Figure 8.6, cells B7 and B8

It's reassuring to see that two very different methods, when they are supposed to do so, agree as closely as results from a Bayesian approach agree with those from a frequentist approach.

Getting Trace Plot Charts

There are several popular methods of diagnosing problems with Markov chains, and one of the most useful is the trace plot chart (see Figure 8.7). You call for a trace plot using a single, simple function:

```
traceplot(model_name)
```

where *model_name* is the name of the model to which the ulam results were assigned.

Figure 8.7
Plot of chains for parameters in the model.

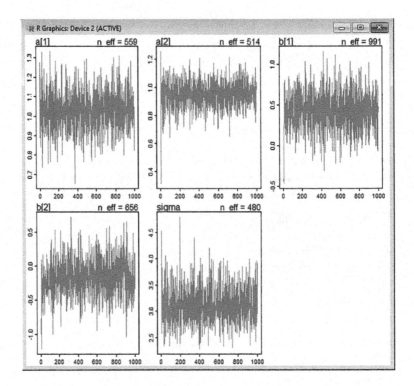

Notice that each trace plot shows the value of a parameter for a different sample. These are reasonably good-looking trace plots. Following the line from left to right, you can see that the line occupies roughly the same area of central tendency across all samples. Although the line rapidly moves across the vertical dimension without getting stuck somewhere, it returns quickly to the central tendency area.

If your trace plot looks very different from those shown here, you could probably get a better sample from ulam. A good place to start is the priors, particularly if you do not have a substantial amount of data in the likelihood. Consider replacing your priors with weakly informative values.

Summary and Concluding Thoughts

Bear in mind that you can use the `ulam` function in place of the other two approaches to Bayesian statistics discussed in this book: grid approximation and quadratic approximation. Those two approaches have drawbacks not shared by MCMC sampling. I spent as much time as I did on them because, conceptually, `quap` builds on grid approximation just as MCMC builds on `quap`.

Most important, you could skip all the material in this book pertaining to distributional features in the data, such as the shape of posterior distributions. You could certainly go directly to R's vignettes, which are well-conceived, and avoid learning about, for example, conjugate priors. But in that case you would not necessarily come away knowing why MCMC works. And if you don't know why it works, you won't know how to fix it when it doesn't.

Way back in the preface to this book, I mentioned that I thought it important for you to know something about the author—particularly so when the book's main topic is subject to considerable contention. The relative merit of two very different approaches to the issue of statistical analysis is bound to result in argument when statisticians discuss it.

It's next door to pointless for me to just tell you, in the context of this book, that I am a frequentist by background and experience. I could promise that I have done my best to treat those two approaches, frequentist and Bayesian, with an even hand, but I know what my promise is worth and you don't. So let's try a different touchstone.

When I was in grad school, my advisor, Gene Glass, was one of the best-known statisticians in the United States. He is responsible for many of the most important advances in frequentist analysis during the second half of the twentieth century. Take the topic of meta-analysis, for example. The basic technique is to restate the means of two or more groups as the difference between those means, divided by the standard deviation of the outcome measure. The result is termed an *effect size*. Across many empirical studies of the same cause, the effect size can be averaged to estimate the effect of that cause. The basic technique had been around and in sporadic use for some time prior to the 1970s. One analyst, in fact, termed a meta-analysis a "study of studies."

But I can still recall seminars, sitting with several other students at Gene's dinner table, watching and listening to him sketch the basics of a formal meta-analysis, its concepts, methods, and terminology (such as "effect size" and the term "meta-analysis" itself). He explained why it was inane to omit primary research that showed "no significant result." It was only a year or so later that his first book on meta-analysis was published, a study of research on different modes of psychotherapy. More books followed, one a meta-analysis of the impact of class size on student achievement and then another on time series analysis.

You couldn't ask for a more thoroughgoing frequentist than Gene was in the 1970s. Then in 1978 Gene attended a colloquium along with other luminaries such as Lee Cronbach, Robert Stake, and Ernest House. (Gene describes this experience in an abbreviated memoir titled *Ghosts and Reminiscences: My Last Day on Earth as a Quantoid*. It can be found in various locations on the Internet.)

Gene writes:

> When questions were being asked I sought to clarify the boundaries that contained Bob's curious thoughts. I asked, "Just to clarify, Bob, between an experimentalist and a person with intimate knowledge of the program in question, who would you trust to produce the most reliable knowledge of the program's efficacy?"

Bob chose the program maven, stunning Gene:

> I insisted that causes could only be known (discovered, found, verified) by randomized, controlled experiments with double-blinding and followed up with statistical significance tests. Ernie and Bob argued that even if you could bring off such an improbable event as the experiment I described, you still wouldn't know what caused a desirable outcome in a particular venue.

Bob and Ernie eventually convinced Gene that their viewpoint was correct:

> They—Bob and Ernie—saw the experimenter as not trained, not capable of the most important step in the chain: conveying to others a sense of what works and how to bring it about.

Carlberg again. I convinced myself somehow that I needed to supplement my bag of frequentist tricks with Bayesian techniques. There are just too many holes in traditional frequentist statistical theory to dismiss the Bayesian approach with a nonchalant wave of the hand. Gene showed that he is capable of reversing his entire point of view as to the value of empirical research. Surely I can reverse my own entire point of view as to a few statistical functions. Can't we all?

Installation Instructions for RStan and the *rethinking* Package on the Windows Platform

A

I wish I didn't have to write this—and that you didn't need to read it—but a variety of issues, such as timing, among others, make it necessary.

Much of this book relies on a package of functions named *rethinking*. These functions help the aspiring Bayesian analyst carry out three basic types of analysis: grid approximation, quadratic approximation, and Markov Chain Monte Carlo. My expectation is that learning to use the functions in the *rethinking* package helps to lay the groundwork for the more complex functionality built into RStan. (RStan is the C++ code that provides an interface between R and the Stan code itself.)

There are a few precautions you should be aware of before taking more than a shallow dive into this book:

- As of the date of this book's publication, the code I supply will not run on a Macintosh computer. Certainly, R itself comes in a version that will run on the Mac, but that version is not designed to use the code in the *rethinking* package.

- You are no doubt familiar with conventions employed on Windows computers. Here I have in mind such characteristics as case sensitivity (R believes that Variable1 and variable1 are two different variables) and the directionality of the slashes between folder names in paths (Windows prefers backslashes, while R prefers forward slashes).

■ Installation of RStan and the *rethinking* package is straightforward but somewhat slow. Fortunately, once it is installed you need not reinstall it unless a version that you can't do without becomes available. The installation that we recommend here works fine at the time of publication.

We assume that you have or will have installed a recent version of R for Windows from the CRAN project site. These are your next steps:

1. Start R. R's console appears.
2. From R's main menu, choose File, New Script.
3. Enter the following code into the new script pane or, if you have a digital version of the code, simply copy and paste it into the new script pane. (The number signs indicate comment lines.)

```
# install rstan from CRAN
install.packages('rstan')
# install cmdstanr from the Stan repository
install.packages("cmdstanr", repos = c("https://mc-stan.org/r-packages/",
getOption("repos")))
# make sure Rtools is installed and setup properly
# this can take a while
cmdstanr::check_cmdstan_toolchain(fix = TRUE)
# then install cmdstanr
# this can take a while too
cmdstanr::install_cmdstan(cores=2)
# install packages from CRAN needed for rethinking
install.packages(c("coda","mvtnorm","devtools","loo","dagitty","shape"))
# install rethinking from GitHub
devtools::install_github("rmcelreath/rethinking")
```

4. With the new script pane still active, choose Run All from the Edit menu. Messages from R will appear in the console.

When the code that runs the installation has completed, you should be ready to go.

Glossary

absolute address

In Excel, the use of a $ prior to a row number and a column letter to lock a formula to that row and column. $C$5 is an absolute address, and if used in a formula it will not change if the formula is copied to a different row or column. C5 is a relative address, and both $C5 and C$5 are mixed addresses.

alist

A list in R that serves as a kind of placeholder. Elements in an alist are not necessarily evaluated immediately but can wait until other elements in the list with a higher priority have been evaluated.

Analysis of Covariance (ANCOVA)

Similar to the Analysis of Variance, ANCOVA adds to the design a numeric variable called a covariate. Before the group means are tested for differences, the correlation between the covariate and the outcome variable is used to adjust the values of the outcome variable.

Analysis of Variance

A test to determine the "statistical significance" of the difference between two (or usually more) group means. The variance between groups is divided by the variance within groups. If this ratio is improbably large, it is concluded that at least two of the group means differ from one another.

autocorrelation

A type of correlation in which, for example, the second value is paired with the first, the third value is paired with the second, the fourth value is paired with the third, and so on. Autocorrelation plays a part in many types of statistical analysis but is particularly useful in time series analysis.

Bayesian

A collection of statistical tests that depend for their validity on a theorem articulated by Thomas Bayes, which defines the relationship between the prior distribution, the likelihood, and the posterior distribution.

BETA.DIST

An Excel function that returns the relative probability of an event when that event is distributed as a continuous variable, given that event's number of successes and failures. Compare with *BETA.INV*.

BETA.INV

An Excel function that returns the frequency of an event when that event is distributed as a continuous variable, given that event's observed successes and failures. Compare with *BETA.DIST*.

BINOM.DIST

An Excel function that returns the relative probability of an event when that event is distributed as a discrete variable, given that event's number of successes and failures. Compare with *BINOM.INV*.

BINOM.INV

An Excel function that returns the frequency of an event when that event is distributed as a discrete variable, given that event's observed successes and failures. Compare with *BINOM.DIST*.

binomial distribution

A distribution that can take on one of only two values; for example, heads and tails for coins, sixes and "not sixes" for dice.

Central Limit Theorem

The expectation that the mean values of many samples will themselves form a normal, Gaussian curve, regardless of the shape of the populations from which the samples were taken.

COMBIN

An Excel function that returns the number of ways to get some number of items from a larger set. Use COMBIN to return the value when you ask it how many ways there are to get 5 clubs from a set of 13 clubs. Often shown as nCr.

compile time error

A software error induced by a mistake in the code itself, such as, in some languages, the use of a variable name without first declaring it.

complete.cases

An R function that returns only the cases in a data frame that have no missing values throughout the data frame's variables.

confidence interval

A range of values of a numeric variable within which a specified portion of cases can be found. The width of the interval is within the analyst's control; for example, a 90% confidence interval on systolic blood pressure might extend from 120 to 130, whereas a 95% confidence interval on the same variable might extend from 110 to 140.

conjugate prior to the likelihood

When a prior and a posterior distribution are of the same distributional family, the prior and the posterior distributions together are termed a conjugate pair. The prior itself can be termed a conjugate prior to the likelihood. When this condition exists, closed form expressions for the posterior become possible, and calculation of integrals may become unnecessary.

continuous variable

A numeric variable whose values bear a meaningful quantitative relationship to one another; for example, degrees Fahrenheit. Compare with *discrete variable*.

correlation

An expression of the relationship between two variables, usually one that requires an observation of one variable to be tied to an observation from the other variable.

correlation coefficient

A measure of the direction and strength of the relationship between variables. It can range from –1 (strong, indirect relationship) to +1 (strong, direct relationship).

critical value

A value of a distribution, such as an F, t, or q distribution, that tells the analyst that an observed statistic is improbable at or beyond that value. The critical value is associated with a probability level selected by the analyst.

data (as a step)

Quantitative information acquired with the intention of combining it with prior information of the same type. Also termed *likelihood*.

data frame

In R, a two-dimensional data structure similar to a table in Excel, subject to various rules (for example, each column should have the same number of data items).

dbeta

An R function that returns the density of a beta distribution, given arguments shape1 and shape2, often construed as successes and failures.

degrees of freedom

The number of values in a set that are themselves free to change without changing a characteristic of the set. If the numbers 1 through 5 constitute a set, then four of those five numbers could change without restriction and the mean of the set would remain the same. The fifth value would of course have to change in order to maintain the mean, but the value of the fifth item would be constrained by the combination of the values of the first four items and the mean itself. The concept of degrees of freedom occurs throughout statistical inference and is one of the most difficult to grasp of the basic inferential concepts.

density

A measure of the relative frequency of a value in a distribution. Compare with *mass*.

determinant

A property of a square matrix that enables tasks such as finding the inverse of a matrix and solving systems of linear equations.

dexp

An R function that returns the density of a value in the exponential distribution.

discrete variable

A variable whose values bear no quantitative relationship to one another. For example, *make of car* includes Ford and Toyota as values, but Ford does not imply a greater amount of "car-ness" than does Toyota. Compare with *continuous variable*.

dnorm

An R function that returns the density of a value in the normal distribution.

dummy coding

A method of identifying group membership by assigning 1s and 0s to groups, resulting in the convenient interpretation of regression coefficients in a multiple regression analysis.

dynamic array formula

A type of array formula in Excel, dating from 2021, that selects on the user's behalf the range that the formula will occupy. Like regular formulas, it is initiated by pressing the Enter key rather than the Ctrl+Shift+Enter sequence.

exponential smoothing

A technique, principally used in time series analysis, that forecasts a new value in a series by means of the relationship between any value in the series and all the preceding values in that series. The influence of each prior value is reduced exponentially as a function of number of intervening observations.

F ratio

The ratio of one variance to another. Most often used in the analysis of variance, where a very large F ratio is taken as evidence of a reliable difference between group means.

factor

(1) A variable, typically measured on a nominal scale, that serves to divide cases according to membership. For example, make-of-car is a possible factor; its values include Ford, Toyota, BMW, and various others. You might want to compare the mean MPG for each value of the make-of-car factor. (2) An unobserved variable that is a composite of observed variables, used in such statistical treatments as factor analysis.

factorial

A sequence of products of consecutive integers in a series. For example, the expression *3 factorial* evaluates to 3 * 2 * 1. The factorial operation is signified by the ! symbol; for example, 3! is shorthand for three factorial.

fixed factor

A fixed factor comprises only those levels of the factor that are of interest to the experimenter, or the only levels that exist. The classification of a factor as fixed or random has implications for how methods such as the analysis of variance are carried out. Compare with *random factor*.

flat prior

A prior that contains a constant value throughout each of its quantiles. See also *noninformative prior*.

frequency distribution

A distribution of values, often shown as a histogram, that has quantiles (or raw counts) on its horizontal axis and a count of the number of observations associated with each particular quantile as its vertical axis.

frequentist

A statistician who makes comparisons between samples and hypothetical populations, using group means as a measure of comparison. By contrast, a Bayesian makes comparisons between samples and populations generated by computer, using probabilities in the appropriate distributions as a measure of comparison.

Gamma function (Γ)

The Gamma function extends the factorial capability, normally used only with integers, to complex numbers.

Gaussian

Pertaining to the normal curve. Named after the contributions made by Carl Gauss to the theory of the normal curve.

homogeneity of variance

An assumption made by certain inferential statistical tests. The assumption is that samples represent populations whose variances are equivalent. The assumption is thought to be largely, if not completely, robust with respect to its violation.

implicit intersection

In Excel, an intersection between two worksheet ranges that do not actually overlap. The intersection is implied by rows or by columns that two ranges have in common. Changes to Excel's formula diction and syntax, made in 2018, enabled this enhancement, along with others such as dynamic array formulas.

index variable

A type of dummy variable.

interaction

In the analysis of variance, it is typical to evaluate two or more factors simultaneously. In a design that evaluates annual income, a researcher might calculate the mean income for males and females, as well as for Republicans and Democrats. Then there would be a main effect for sex and another main effect for political party. There would also be an interaction effect with four cells: female Democrats, female Republicans, male Democrats, and male Republicans. Interactions are not limited to two factors, however. Interactions between continuous variables, particularly in Bayesian statistics, are plausible and useful.

intercept

(Often referred to as the *constant*.) The intercept is the point where the regression line crosses a chart's Y axis, and therefore where the products of the regression coefficients and their associated predictor variables are zero.

inverse (of a matrix)

In matrix algebra, when Matrix A is pre- or post-multiplied by Matrix B, if the resulting matrix has the numeral 1 in each main diagonal cell and 0 elsewhere, Matrix A and Matrix B are inverses of one another.

leapfrogging

Steps that a sampler takes to most effectively cover a posterior distribution are termed leapfrog steps.

least squares regression

A method of quantifying the relationship between a predicted variable and one or more predictor variables, in which the criterion is met when the sum of the squared deviations between the predicted and actual values is minimized.

`library` function

An R function that instructs R to make available an installed package of functions that together achieve a particular quantitative purpose.

likelihood

The acquisition of new data subsequent to the establishment of a prior and before the calculation of a new posterior.

LINEST

An Excel function that carries out least squares regression.

`lm`

An R function that carries out least squares regression.

logarithm (log)

The power to which a base is raised to result in a particular number.

Markov Chain Monte Carlo (MCMC)

A relatively fast method of generating samples from a posterior distribution via sampling methods that employ user-specified distributional characteristics, such as measures of central tendency and spread.

mass

A measure of the area (usually expressed as a percentage) under a curve and delimited by two points on the horizontal axis. Compare with *density*.

matrix algebra

A collection of tools that enables the manipulation of matrices in much the same way that simple arithmetic manipulates individual numbers. Typical operations in matrix algebra include matrix multiplication, matrix inversion, matrix transposition, and the calculation of determinants.

mean

The arithmetical average. The total of a set of values divided by the number of such values.

multicollinearity

A condition in which two or more predictor variables in a regression equation are perfectly or very closely correlated. Using traditional matrix algebra techniques, this condition causes nonsensical regression results, such as negative values for R^2.

multiple comparisons

Several techniques, usually employed after an ANOVA, designed to identify which group means in the ANOVA are significantly different from one another.

multiple regression

Linear regression using two or more independent variables and a single dependent variable.

nCr

Formulaic shorthand for a function that returns the number of ways to combine N things, R things at a time.

noninformative prior

See *flat prior*.

NORM.S.INV

An Excel function that returns a quantile from the standard normal curve, given a probability level supplied by the user.

normal (or Gaussian) distribution

The so-called bell curve, characterized by a single measure of central tendency (the mean) and a single measure of spread (the standard deviation or variance). The normal distribution describes many different variables, including the mean values of several other distributional shapes.

null hypothesis

A hypothesis that assumes there is no post-treatment difference, other than a design flaw such as sampling error, between two or more groups when they have been initially equated by random selection and assignment.

parameter

In traditional frequentist statistics, a parameter is calculated on a population, whereas a statistic is calculated on a sample. The parameter cannot be observed directly, if only because the population has changed during the data acquisition. In Bayesian statistics the parameter still cannot be observed but it's identified as the value with the maximum posterior probability.

pbinom

An R function that returns a cumulative probability from the binomial distribution, given a quantile or a vector of quantiles, the number of trials, and the probability of success on any given trial.

p-hacking

The disreputable practice of selecting a particular data analysis technique, or a particular subset of the available data, in order to artificially inflate the apparent statistical significance of the findings.

PI function

A rethinking function that returns the highest probability mass for a given percentile interval in a sample.

pipe symbol

A vertical bar |, used principally in R as a separator in an argument list.

planned orthogonal contrasts

A multiple comparison technique, characterized by the specification of variable coefficients prior to the collection of data, such that the coefficients are uncorrelated to one another. More statistically powerful than the alternatives but still not especially powerful.

posterior distribution

A distribution of values returned by R, the result of combining a prior distribution with a likelihood distribution.

precis

A function in the rethinking package that creates a summary table of estimates, standard deviations, and correlations between parameters in a given model, often one produced by the quap or the ulam functions.

predictor variable

A variable in a regression equation that bears a quantifiable relationship to the equation's outcome variable and that contributes to the accuracy of the predictive equation.

prior

A Bayesian analysis must include an initial estimate of the probability of each value of each parameter. These estimates are collectively termed "the prior."

probability density function (PDF)

A measurement that expresses the height of a curve at a given quantile relative to the height of the curve at other quantiles.

probability mass function (PMF)

A measurement that expresses the amount of area under a curve as a percent of the total area under the curve.

qbinom

An R function that returns a vector of quantiles when it is supplied with a vector of probabilities, number of trials, the size of each trial, and the probability of success on each trial.

quadratic approximation

A posterior distribution that resembles a normal or Gaussian curve.

quantile

A method of dividing a distribution into equally spaced components. A quantile is a general-purpose term for percentiles, deciles, and quartiles.

quap

A rethinking function that returns a Gaussian posterior distribution according to specifications supplied by the user.

R^2

A method of calculating the best relationship between a predicted variable and one or more predictor variables that minimizes the total of the squared deviations between the predicted and the actual observations.

random factor

A factor whose levels are selected at random from a larger population of factor levels. The factor *hospital* and the factor *patient* would normally be considered random factors. An experiment might include both fixed and random factors, and the statistical treatment of the data from such an experiment would differ from a treatment that uses only fixed factors.

ratio variables

Continuous variables that have a true zero point, such as degrees kelvin.

rbinom

An R function that returns random values from a binomial distribution.

regression

A type of statistical analysis that depends heavily on the use of correlations between predictor variables and predicted variables. Regression is a standard method used with the general linear model, and it can be used in place of other well-known types of analysis, such as the t-test and the analysis of variance.

regression coefficient

A coefficient for a predictor variable in a regression equation that helps the full equation minimize the squared deviations between the observed and the predicted values.

relative address

A means of addressing a cell in an Excel worksheet. If the cell is copied and pasted to a different cell in the worksheet, any cells addressed by means of a relative address adjust their row and/or column accordingly. Compare with *absolute address*.

rep function

An R function that returns a user-supplied number of replicates of a given value.

rethinking package

A collection of functions that can be installed and executed on a personal computer. The functions are designed to bridge the gap between an analyst's knowledge of the distributional and relational characteristics of the variables of interest, and the syntax of functions defined and recognized in the RStan programming language. As such, many of these functions can be thought of as "helper" or "wrapper" functions. Designed and written by Richard McElreath.

sample

An R function that returns random samples from a vector such as a probability grid.

Scheffé

A multiple comparisons method, capable of post hoc comparisons and complex contrasts such as the mean of two groups against the mean of three other groups. The most conservative of the recognized multiple contrast procedures.

scope

In Excel, a name can refer to a cell or a range of cells on a worksheet. The name can be defined as belonging to a particular worksheet or to a workbook as a whole. That is the name's scope. In VBA, variables can be defined at the module level or at the procedure level. The location at which the variable is declared determines the variable's scope.

seq function

An R function that generates an equidistant sequence of numeric values, given a start value, a stop value, and the number of values to generate.

setwd function

An R function that specifies the working directory that R will use to read data files and to write output.

skewed

A variable whose distribution is asymmetric is said to be skewed.

slope

The gradient of a regression line. The degree of change in the regression line's vertical position for every unit of change in its horizontal position. In a multiple regression context it is probably more accurate to refer to a predictor's coefficient than to its slope.

Solver

A VBA utility for Excel that derives the minimum, maximum, or specified value of a precedent, given the desired value of a consequence. Similar to but more complex than Excel's Goal Seek tool.

standard deviation

The square root of the average squared deviation between each value in the set and the mean of those values. It is a convenient and standard measure of a value's location in a distribution, particularly a Gaussian distribution, which is completely defined by its mean and degree of spread.

standard error of estimate

The standard deviation of the difference between observed values and the values that are predicted by a regression equation.

standard error of intercept

The standard deviation associated with a regression equation's intercept or constant. Useful in evaluating the distance between the reported intercept and 0.

standard error of the mean

The standard deviation of group means. In frequentist methods, the standard error of the mean is often estimated from one group mean by dividing a sample standard deviation by the square root of the sample size.

Str

An R function that summarizes structural information about individual variables in an R object, such as a data frame.

strong prior

A prior distribution based on so many cases that a likelihood is unlikely to move the posterior distribution far from the prior.

sum of squares and cross products (SSCP)

A matrix used in matrix algebra that shows sums of squares in the main diagonal and sums of cross products in the off diagonal cells.

Tibble

An R utility that reformats a summary of results into a table that is more visually attractive and informative than a standard results summary.

trace plot

A line chart that shows the samples produced by, for example, a Markov chain, plotted in sequential order. Trace plots are useful in diagnosing problems with Markov chains.

t-test

A statistical test, often but by no means always of the difference between two mean values. Typically, a t-test divides a statistic such as the difference between two means by the standard error of that statistic. If the variability between group means is improbably large compared to the variability between individual cases, the analyst may conclude that the difference between

the means is a reliable one. A t-test may also be used as a test of the difference between a regression coefficient and zero.

Type I error

A Type I error causes the analyst to conclude that a treatment has had an effect when in fact it has not. A false positive.

Type II error

A Type II error causes the analyst to conclude that a treatment has had *no* effect when in fact it has had one. A false negative.

ulam

A helper function in the rethinking package that provides the necessary information for RStan to generate a model and draw samples from that model. Stan Ulam was an Austrian mathematician who contributed much to the development of MCMC models.

uniform (rectangular) distribution

A uniform distribution has a constant value in all its quantiles. This makes it particularly useful for designating the spread of a parameter: standard deviations are constant across quantiles.

uniform prior

A uniform prior assigns the same value to all the quantiles in a prior.

variance

The average squared difference between the mean of a set of values and each individual value in that set. The square root of the variance is the standard deviation. With small sample sizes, bias in the variance is removed by dividing by the count minus one, rather than by the count exactly. In this context, the quantity "count minus one" is referred to as "degrees of freedom."

warmup

An early phase of the work done by a sampler to determine the step size needed to cover the posterior most efficiently.

weak prior

A weak prior has so few values in its quantiles that the prior has virtually no effect on a posterior distribution, because of the effect of combining the prior with a much larger likelihood.

z-score

A z-score, or standard score, subtracts the mean of a set of scores from an observed score and divides that difference by the set's standard deviation. It tells you immediately whether a given score is above or below the mean and the number of standard deviations separating that score from the mean.

Index

Symbols

A

B

VIDEO TRAINING FOR THE **IT PROFESSIONAL**

LEARN QUICKLY
Learn a new technology in just hours. Video training can teach more in less time, and material is generally easier to absorb and remember.

WATCH AND LEARN
Instructors demonstrate concepts so you see technology in action.

TEST YOURSELF
Our Complete Video Courses offer self-assessment quizzes throughout.

CONVENIENT
Most videos are streaming with an option to download lessons for offline viewing.

Learn more, browse our store, and watch free, sample lessons at
informit.com/video

Save 50%* off the list price of video courses with discount code **VIDBOB**

Register Your Product at informit.com/register

Access additional benefits and save up to 65%* on your next purchase

- Automatically receive a coupon for 35% off books, eBooks, and web editions and 65% off video courses, valid for 30 days. Look for your code in your InformIT cart or the Manage Codes section of your account page.

- Download available product updates.

- Access bonus material if available.**

- Check the box to hear from us and receive exclusive offers on new editions and related products.

InformIT—The Trusted Technology Learning Source

InformIT is the online home of information technology brands at Pearson, the world's leading learning company. At informit.com, you can

- Shop our books, eBooks, and video training. Most eBooks are DRM-Free and include PDF and EPUB files.

- Take advantage of our special offers and promotions (informit.com/promotions).

- Sign up for special offers and content newsletter (informit.com/newsletters).

- Access thousands of free chapters and video lessons.

- Enjoy free ground shipping on U.S. orders.*

* Offers subject to change.
** Registration benefits vary by product. Benefits will be listed on your account page under Registered Products.

Connect with InformIT—Visit informit.com/community

 twitter.com/informit

 Pearson

Addison-Wesley • Adobe Press • Cisco Press • Microsoft Press • Oracle Press • Peachpit Press • Pearson IT Certification • Que

How to Access the Companion Content Files

Register your purchase of the print edition of Bayesian Analysis with Excel and R to access online workbooks and the companion ebook.

Follow these steps:

1. Go to **informit.com/register** and log in or create a new account.

2. Enter the ISBN: **9780137580989**

3. Click on the "Access Bonus Content" link in the Registered Products section of your account page. This will take you to the page where your downloadable content is available.
